How to Retire H

How to Retire Happy

Everything You Need to Know About the 12 Most Important Decisions You Must Make Before You Retire

Stan Hinden

McGraw-Hill

New York San Francisco Washington, D.C. Auckland Bogotá
Caracas Lisbon London Madrid Mexico City Milan
Montreal New Delhi San Juan Singapore
Sydney Tokyo Toronto

McGraw-Hill

A Division of The **McGraw·Hill** Companies

5 6 7 8 9 0   DOC/DOC   0 6 5 4 3 2

ISBN 0-07-136034-4

Printed and bound by R. R. Donnelley & Sons Company.

This publication is designed to provide accurate and authoritative information in regard to the subject matter covered. It is sold with the understanding that neither the author nor the publisher is engaged in rendering legal, accounting, or other professional service. If legal advice or other expert assistance is required, the services of a competent professional person should be sought.
*—From a Declaration of Principles jointly adopted
by a Committee of the American Bar
Association and a Committee of Publishers*

McGraw-Hill books are available at special quantity discounts to use as premiums and sales promotions, or for use in corporate training programs. For more information, please write to the Director of Special Sales, Professional Publishing, McGraw-Hill, Two Penn Plaza, New York, NY 10121-2298. Or contact your local bookstore.

 This book is printed on recycled, acid-free paper containing a minimum of 50% recycled de-inked fiber.

For Sara,
who made the journey with me.

Contents

Foreword

Congratulations! You are about to read a wonderful, sensible, and simple book that will be a priceless asset to you. If you're thinking about retiring, or have decided to retire within the next several years, or have decided not to retire just yet—or even if you retired some years ago—Stan Hinden's book will help you analyze the 12 vital decisions you must make at retirement as well as offer expert advice in each area—and do so in words that are easy to read, bereft of financial jargon and gobbledygook.

I happen to be in the category "not ready to retire." While I'm chronologically 71 years of age, measured by the age of the heart that was transplanted into my chest nearly five years ago, I'm a mere child of 30. I love my work too much to stop just yet. But I've already personally considered many of the decisions Stan discusses and will be that much better prepared when (and if!) I finally decide to retire.

Most of my own expertise, such as it may be, is in the world of finance. My entire career of a near-half century has been in the mutual fund industry, and I fully endorse just about every one of Stan Hinden's recommendations about investing for, and in, retirement. To afford a comfortable retirement, for example, *does* depend on the power of time and is greatly facilitated by using tax-efficient mutual funds, a breed that remains all too rare today.

Social Security is a critical part of retirement income for most families. Although we can't control the schedule of benefits, we *can* control the time when our payments begin;, and the advice this book gives is good: The longer you wait (up to age 70), the larger the check you'll receive. While Social Security is designed to provide a minimal standard for retirement income, its stream of benefits can be estimated to have a capital value of some $300,000 at age 70. That value is even better than it looks, for it is the equivalent of a fixed-income investment, with a built-in hedge against inflation—two priceless assets when you retire.

Stan Hinden's book is also right on the mark in its chapters about making decisions on company pensions, 401(k) corporate thrift plans, and individual retirement accounts. His advice benefits greatly from his firsthand experience (some derived from his own investment mistakes) as he presents wisdom on investing during retirement—virtually all of which I heartily endorse. His five "Golden Rules" are, well, golden. Yet they are so simple and basic that too many investors give no attention to them and pay the consequences. And his advice on asset allocation and the need for significant holdings in bonds or annuities to produce income is also well worth heeding.

Stan recognizes that a successful retirement requires much more than a successful investment program. His chapters on health insurance, preparing for illness, deciding where you want to live, and estate planning present a whole variety of ideas, many of which I had never given much consideration. But I'm considering them now. And in his final chapter—on successful aging—he gives all of us in the sixties, seventies, and eighties age group a marvelous compendium of good advice, including how to maintain our physical and mental energies, some tricks we can use when memory fails (yes, it happens to me, too), and how to remain actively engaged in the great game of life.

This is a great book because it fills a major gap in the investment literature. There are countless books about accumulating financial assets for retirement, but few about what to do when you get there, and Stan's book offers as intelligent and comprehensive an approach as I've seen. It takes a great deal of the mystery and confusion out of retirement and, by so doing, allays much of the anxiety you may feel as the time approaches.

To say Stan Hinden is well qualified to write a book on retirement is something like saying Tiger Woods is well-qualified to hold a golf clinic. First, as the saying goes, Stan has "been there, done that." He's traded in his remarkable career as a successful journalist, retiring from his job as a financial columnist for the *Washington Post* in 1996, and has five years of retirement under his belt. Although he's clearly remained active and productive, obviously investing a large amount of time into writing this book ("having it both ways," as the author puts it), he knows where the challenges and opportunities lie.

With his firsthand experience in retirement, his journalist's gift for simple writing, and his considerable financial expertise, Stan Hinden has carried off with considerable success the challenge of helping those of us considering or experiencing retirement. In *How to Retire Happy: Everything You Need to Know about the 12 Most Important Decisions You Must Make Before You Retire*, he has done so with flair and common sense. I am confident that his wisdom will improve your own preparation for retirement and help all of us who take the opportunity this book presents to consider his helpful and constructive advice.

John C. Bogle
Valley Forge, Pennsylvania
August 1, 2000

Preface

This is the book I wish I had been able to read before I retired. If I had, my monthly Social Security check would be fatter. My company pension would be better. My retirement savings account would be significantly larger. And I'd have a better chance of making my money last during what I hope will be a long retirement.

But that's not all. If I had known what I know now, I would have been better prepared, both psychologically and emotionally, for my retirement. I also would have had a keener appreciation for the life-enhancing opportunities and experiences that retirement can bring you.

I retired from the *Washington Post* in 1996. I was then 69 years old and had spent 23 years at the *Post*—the last 12 years as a financial columnist—writing about stocks and mutual funds. All told, I spent about 45 years in journalism as a reporter, writer, and editor.

Several months after I retired, I began writing a column for the *Post* called "Retirement Journal," which chronicled my experiences as a retiree. In essence, this book is the story of my retirement: what I learned and what I think you should know about the subject. My goal is to take the mystery out of retirement and to reduce the confusion that many retirees feel.

Shortly after I left my full-time job, I realized that I was woefully unprepared to make many of the decisions that are required of a retiree. I knew little, if anything, about Social Security, medicare, medigap, medicare HMOs, long-term-care, mandatory IRA withdrawals, pensions, and so on. But even though I was uninformed, I had to make far-reaching personal decisions on all of those subjects. Inevitably, as you will read, I made some bad decisions and learned some costly lessons.

The job of writing a regular column about my retirement experiences opened a window for me on a part of life that I had not known much about or even thought much about. Indeed, the more I learned, the more convinced I became that preparation and knowledge are the keys to a happy retirement.

It has been said that retirement is not an event, but a process. If so, that process should begin long before you turn in your retirement papers. It is simply not logical to expect that you can learn all you need to know to make major retirement decisions in a few days, or even a few weeks, as I tried to do.

So consider this book a reporter's firsthand report from the front lines of retirement. My hope is that this easy-reader tour will help future retirees better prepare for the day when they stop working full time. I also hope the book will help current retirees find ways to improve their retirement experiences.

Retirement in America was once a casual, even a drab, "You're over the hill" experience. It was a sign that the retiree was nearing the end of his or her productive life and was even getting close to the end of life itself.

Today, retirement in America has changed dramatically. It has become an upbeat, full-speed-ahead, "let's-start-a-second-career" experience, made possible by longer life spans, tax-deferred savings plans, and government-sponsored income and health programs.

How to Retire Happy has 12 chapters, each one dealing with one of the 12 key decisions retirees must make during the retirement process.

Some of the decisions are related to our attitudes toward life and work and the complex emotions that surround retirement. We are faced with many questions: How we feel about leaving our long-time friends and colleagues at work, how we feel about relocating to a new community, and even how we feel about growing older.

Some of our other decisions involve the web of government programs and regulations that affect all retirees. They include the age at which we take our Social Security payments, the way we manage our health care, and even how we make our mandatory IRA withdrawals when we reach age 70½. You don't have to be a rocket scientist to figure out your withdrawals—although it would help.

Finally, there are the financial decisions that will determine whether you will have a comfortable or an uncomfortable retirement. I often think about that old saying, "I've been rich and I've been poor. Rich is better." Smart saving and investing can make the difference. But as the book points out, you will have to work at it.

Retirement is not a simple matter. But your retirement decisions will be a lot easier if you take the time to understand your choices. Then you can start having fun. A happy retirement is within everybody's reach. The time to start is now. The place to start is here.

Stan Hinden

ACKNOWLEDGMENTS

My thanks go first to David Ignatius, the executive editor of the *International Herald Tribune*. David was the assistant managing editor/business at the *Washington Post* in 1996, when I retired from my job as a financial columnist. It was at his suggestion that I began to write a new column called "Retirement Journal," a first-person report on my experiences as a retiree. His encouragement and support were crucial to the success of the column, which led to this book.

I also had wonderful support for my column from the executives, editors, and writers at the *Post*. Special thanks go to Assistant Managing Editor/Business Jill Dutt, Deputy Business Editor Thomas F. Dimond, Business Researcher Richard Drezen, and Kate Carlisle, managing editor (Washington) of the *Los Angeles Times-Washington Post* News Service, which sends my "Retirement Journal" column to newspapers around the world.

The key to any successful journey is having a good guide to show you the sights. On my journey through the land of retirement, I have had many excellent guides.

At the Social Security Administration, my guides included Commissioner Kenneth S. Apfel and his aides in the press office, notably

Press Officer Catherine L. Noe, Public Information Specialist Carolyn J. Cheezum, and John B. Trollinger, former deputy press officer.

My guide through the jungle of estate planning was Attorney Rhonda J. Macdonald. I am grateful for her infinite patience and meticulous attention to detail. I am also grateful to my friend, financial planner Jack R. May, who helped me analyze many of the investment concepts in this book.

Helping me find my way through the maze called "required minimum distributions"—the money you must take out of your IRA accounts—were a group of experts that included Christine S. Fahlund, financial planner, T. Rowe Price Associates; Ellen Breslow, managing director, Individual Retirement and Financial Planning Services, Salomon Smith Barney; and two Vanguard Group experts, John E. Barth, principal, Retirement Services Group, and Frank Eliason, retirement specialist.

My thanks also go to Melissa Gannon, vice president, Weiss Ratings, Inc., of Palm Beach Gardens, Florida, for her help with medigap and long-term care statistics; and to Charles F. Mondin, director of communications and marketing, United Seniors Health Cooperative. At AARP, I had help from John Rother, director of legislation and public policy; and media specialists Steven Hahn and Thomas H. Otwell.

I am especially grateful for the encouragement that this book received from Lisa Swayne of the The Swayne Agency and Mary E. Glenn, my editor at McGraw-Hill. My son, Lawrence H. Hinden, and my daughter, Pamela S. Hinden, have heartened me with their enthusiasm for my writings. They both made very valuable editing suggestions. I also appreciate the editing and technical help I received from Dr. Denice Rothman.

My wife, Sara, to whom I have been married for 47 years, not only shared my retirement experiences, but provided many thoughtful ideas about the manuscript as well. Sara was also kind enough to never ask why a retired writer keeps writing.

S. H.

DECISION 1

Am I ready to retire?

Are you ready to retire?

When the stress levels at work are unbearable, it's easy to be flippant and shout, "You bet I'm ready to retire. Let me out of here!"

At such moments, it's also easy to fantasize about all the things you could do if you didn't have to go to work every day. You can see yourself soaking up the sun on a tropical beach, whiling away the hours on a golf course, or having gobs of time to read, watch movies, or trade stocks on-line.

You think about all the things you've wanted to do, but never had time for: a cruise around the Greek islands, a tour of Australia and New Zealand, watching the bullfights in Spain, or enjoying Carnaval in Brazil.

And then you suddenly realize you could even buy a season ticket for your local baseball team and go to games in the middle of the week! What a luxury!

It's also quite wonderful to think about the things you could give up: all your bosses, all those memos, and all those boring meetings. Gone, too, from your life would be those rush-hour traffic jams and the frustrations of your daily commute. If your job requires you to travel, you could stop bouncing around in airplanes and trying to sleep on lumpy hotel-room pillows.

As a retired person, you'd be free to make your own schedule, to do what you want, and go where you want when you want. Ah, freedom!

But wait! Remember, the old adage: If it sounds too good to be true, it probably is. Like a lot of daydreams, these visions of retirement may or may not be realistic. They may not even be what you really want when you retire.

The fact is that when you face the question "Am I ready to retire?" your answer may have little to do with your fantasies and a lot more to do with your age, your health, your family, the nature of your job, your financial situation, and your outlook on life.

So to be realistic, let's look at the pros and cons of whether you are ready to retire. We'll discuss three good reasons for retiring and three equally good reasons for not retiring.

Then we'll talk about people who have it both ways: They retire and—guess what?—they go back to work, usually part time. As people live longer and healthier lives, the part-time option is becoming more and more popular.

We'll also look at what life is like for married couples after they retire. And we'll talk about the psychological impact of retirement—how you can go from a busy, even frantic, working life to a laid-back, but productive, retirement.

Three good reasons for retiring

Reason one: The time is right

If there is "a time under the sun for everything," then surely there is a time in your life when you can look in the mirror and rightfully tell yourself, "I've worked hard all my life. I've met every challenge life has thrown at me. It's time for me to stop working and to start living life my own way. These are the years that belong to me."

If this is how you truly feel, that's fine. Once you retire, you'll be free to shape your life in a manner that gives you the greatest satisfaction and happiness. But to make the most of your new freedom, you'll need a plan.

In a way, retiring is like going on a trip abroad. You wouldn't just pack a suitcase and board a plane. You'd try to prepare for your journey. You'd read guidebooks about the places you plan to visit, study currency exchange rates, and find out what kind of weather to expect. And, of course, you'd prepare an itinerary so you'd know where you were going and when.

Similarly, if you want your journey into retirement to be successful, you must do two things: First, equip yourself with the information you'll need on your journey into the world of Social Security, Medicare, medigap, long-term care, pensions, and 401(k) plans. Second, decide what you want to do in retirement.

Doing nothing is not a viable option for most people. Studies show that people who retire from active careers and become couch potatoes often suffer from depression and other ills associated with feeling useless and unwanted.

Your retirement plan can take many forms. You can spend your time improving your golf or tennis game, coaching a kids' soccer or baseball team, working for a service club such as the Lions or Kiwanis, or volunteering for a charitable or community organization. Many retirees enjoy spending time with their children and grandchildren. I know I do.

Retirement is a great time to complete some of your long-delayed personal projects. You may want to take some college courses, learn to play a musical instrument, or try your hand at writing mystery novels or painting. Many retirees—even those starting at late ages—demonstrate unusual creativity and artistic skills.

Whatever you decide to do in retirement, your plan should have one main objective: to keep yourself mentally and physically active and in close contact with other people. That is the way to achieve a successful retirement.

Reason two: You've got more compelling things to do

As we age and gain experience, we often find that our goals in life become clearer. So it was with my friend, Jane Hoden. Religion, faith, and community service had long been the cornerstones of her life. And inwardly, she knew that when she retired some day, she would find a way to fulfill her personal commitment to be of service to others.

"I believe God has a plan for our lives, which is revealed in time," Jane says.

"This past year," Jane recalled, "my mother lived with us. It gave us great insight into what life is like for a person who is elderly, has significant health and financial issues, and feels that life is not within [her] control."

Jane said she soon realized that while churches focus on the needs of youth, the newly married, or active adults, they rarely address the needs of seniors. The more Jane studied the problem, the more she became convinced that forming a ministry for seniors was destined to be her calling in retirement.

So, in the year 2000, Jane, who is 55, retired from the federal government, where she had worked for 31 years as a public information specialist and, most recently, as the manager of the news division in her agency. Her government pension was reduced somewhat because she took "early retirement." But she didn't believe money would be a problem. Her husband, Paul, is a retired Air Force colonel with his own pension, and he works part time as a consultant.

"We looked at his income and at my income in retirement, at our savings and our expenses, and we decided we could afford for me to retire," Jane said.

To enjoy an active retirement and pursue Jane's ministry for seniors, the couple moved to Virginia Beach, Virginia, where they soon began their efforts at the Wycliffe Presbyterian Church.

What is Jane's goal? Not to replicate many of the excellent social services already available to seniors. Rather, she says, her mission "is to be a presence for retirees who need a connection to people who will provide support and caring." Jane believes that she and other volunteers can brighten the lives of many seniors who are lonely and isolated.

Retiring at 55 was "a golden opportunity," Jane says. "I'm still young enough to make a contribution for another decade." She likes the idea of doing just that.

Reason three: Your job is changing

My friend Larry, who is a scientist, retired from the federal government after 35 years. He was age 60 when he decided to leave. He told me that he was undecided about retiring quite that early, but organizationally, his agency was in a state of flux that he felt was not personally satisfying.

A year before he left, Larry said, potential budget cutbacks had caused major personnel reassignments in the agency; he had been moved to a position that was far afield from his specialty. In addition, old-timers were being encouraged to leave with buyouts.

So he assessed his situation and tried to figure out whether he could afford to retire. He decided he could. His government pension would be about 45 percent of his salary, and in two years he would be eligible for a small monthly Social Security benefit because he had taught college classes part time for many years. He also would continue to earn money from teaching, and he planned to accept a three-year research fellowship that paid fairly well. "The money and research combined made it interesting," he said of the fellowship. So, at that point, Larry said, it seemed like a good time to leave. And he did.

"It was time for me to be unhooked from an unchallenging position and to get more involved in what really interested me, which was teaching and scientific study," Larry said.

Today, Larry is doing what he wanted to do. He is teaching at a local college 12 hours a week and working on technology projects as part of his fellowship. And, he says, he's happy to be "retired."

Three good reasons for not retiring

Reason one: You like working

It sounds contradictory: You can be ready to retire, but not ready to give up work. What does that mean? It means that work is a habit that is hard to break. As strange as it may seem, especially on those dreadful days when everything goes wrong, work is an integral and even necessary part of our lives.

Many of us began working as teenagers and have never really stopped. In our early years, our jobs provided the money that made it possible for us to pay for the necessities of life. Later on, our work made it possible for us to pay for some of the luxuries of life. But for most of us, the meaning of work goes far beyond our paychecks. Our jobs and careers have given us our greatest challenges and our highest achievements. Our careers have helped us find our role in society. And for better or worse, our work has become our identity.

Soon after I retired, I began having identity problems. For 23 years, I had been calling people on the telephone and saying, "This is Stan Hinden of *The Washington Post*." After I left the newspaper, when I made a phone call I was just "Stan Hinden," and I felt I had lost a piece of my identity.

This problem sometimes cropped up at social gatherings where I would meet people for the first time. At these affairs, people often look for conversational openings by asking each other, "What kind of work do you do?" In American life, it is common for people to measure the worth and value of other people by their work and titles. This tendency is unfortunate, but it happens all the time.

After I retired and people asked me what kind of work I did, I tended to stumble. I found myself saying, "Well, I'm retired. But I *used to be* a writer at *The Washington Post*." The phrase "used to be" didn't come easily to my lips. It was like saying, "I'm a has-been." And I didn't like that feeling one bit.

Thus, I found that not only did retirement tamper with my identity and my image of myself, but it put me in a "has-been" category that was uncomfortable for someone who had led a vigorous working life.

Reason two: You'll miss the people you work with

The idea of not having to go to your job every day may seem mighty attractive, but ask yourself this question:

"Am I really ready to give up working and everything that goes with it?" That "everything" includes not only the challenges and frustrations of your job, but also the familiar, and even welcome, daily routines at work.

Ask yourself also, "Will I miss the people I work with?"

These are not facetious questions. Although we like to scoff at the idea that we love our jobs, work plays an important role in our lives. It provides us with a sense of purpose and accomplishment and, of course, a place to go in the morning. For many of us, our job site is our home away from home, the place where we spend time with a network of friends and colleagues.

That network tends to dissolve quickly when you retire and step out of the working world, as I found when I retired from *The Washington Post* after a 45-year career as a reporter, editor, and columnist. So it's not surprising to me that many retirees say they miss work—or at least the friends and shared experiences they had at work.

This sense of loss hit me after I retired from my job as a financial writer at the *Post* and before I went back to writing part time. It took me quite a while to figure out why—even though I loved retirement—I seemed to miss working. I was puzzled.

I knew, of course, why I liked retirement: It gave me that wonderful sense of freedom I mentioned earlier. After 45 years of working, it was delightful to be able to live by my own timetable. But why then did I miss working? Eventually, it dawned on me that what I really missed was not my *work*, but my *workplace*.

My office had been my second home, a place where I could chat with friends, catch up on gossip, swap office rumors, and help the other Monday morning quarterbacks decide what to do with the Washington Redskins. When I left the paper, I left all that behind. And I missed it.

Reason three: You don't have anything else you'd rather do

My friend Hy Avrut, who is 80, owns his own business and still goes to work every day. When I ask him why he doesn't retire, he says, "I don't know what I would do with myself." Hy is a man without hobbies, and after 55 years of running his own business, he says he has no appetite for spending his time in shopping centers. He recently agreed to take off Wednesdays so he could play golf. But he says that if he retired, he would miss the interaction with his customers and even the headaches of his business.

Hy puts it this way: "I'm healthy and energetic, and I want to stay busy. Regardless of what the calendar says, I'm still able to do what I've done all these years. Maybe one of these days I will have to slow down. But right now I'm doing fine."

Retiring and working: Having it both ways

The line between work and retirement is becoming more blurred all the time. The fact is that many people who retire go back to work part time—some even full time. People are living longer and want to remain involved and productive.

Several of my retired friends have gone back to work part time or full time.

Bill Backer retired after 38 years at General Electric and then went back to work at GE under the company's Golden Opportunity program, which allows retirees to work up to 1000 hours a year. A marketing specialist, Bill works about 500 hours a year, helping GE organize a customer conference.

Now 74, Bill has worked part time for 12 years and continues to be enthusiastic about the job. "I have long-standing friendships where I work . . . and I have a kinship with the business," he says.

My friend Jerry Goldberg, who is 73, works full time as a school-bus driver in Montgomery County, Maryland. Before he retired, Jerry spent 30 years in the dry-cleaning business. Jerry says he enjoys driving and gets along well with the schoolchildren. He likes the health and vacation benefits that come with his job and his pay. He gets about $13 an hour and works a 40-hour week during the school year. He's happy with his job. "I expect to keep it for two to three years, providing I stay well. It keeps me going, and I always look forward to the next day," he says.

Backer and Goldberg are only the advance guard of a huge wave of future retirees who say they plan to work at least part time.

Two recent national surveys show that we can expect an explosion of part-time retired workers in the years ahead. That's because members of the baby-boom generation—77 million people born between 1946 and 1964—will begin to retire in 2010.

The first survey, conducted by the Gallup Organization for the brokerage firm PaineWebber, Inc., reported that 85 percent of boomers plan to continue working after retirement.

In the second survey, taken by Roper Starch Worldwide, Inc., for AARP, 80 percent of boomers indicated that they planned to work at least part time after retirement.

In both surveys, relatively small numbers of people said they expected to work because they needed the money; most said they wanted to keep busy or pursue individual goals. A significant number of people indicated that they wanted to start their own businesses.

Retirees already make up a significant portion of the temporary workforce at Interim Services, Inc., of Fort Lauderdale, Florida, a $4.3 billion-a-year international staffing company.

Raymond Marcy, the company's president, told me that 15.5 percent of the firm's 700,000 employees are retirees who work part time, up from 12 percent four years ago. He expects that percentage to continue to grow. "Many retirees," he said, "are in great health; they want to stay active, and they're energetic."

Working as temps, retirees often become prized employees, Marcy noted, because they're mature and they approach their jobs with the sort of patience and perspective that employers are looking for.

"Up until very recently," Marcy told me, "there was a very bright line between working full time and retirement."

But that line, Marcy added, is now blurred as seniors increasingly decide how many hours or weeks a year they want to work and how they want to balance their professional and personal lives.

According to Marcy, what was once a black or white condition—work versus retirement—has been transformed into many shades of gray. "The flexibility you have now is truly incredible," Marcy said.

He noted that a 1999 survey conducted by Interim Services, in conjunction with Louis Harris & Associates, concluded that early baby boomers—those over age 53—ranked higher on job satisfaction and company loyalty than did the generation Xers who are succeeding them in the labor force.

The report stated, "Maturity in terms of years of experience and age seem to bring about greater satisfaction with one's career. With significant labor shortages today and in the future...older workers will become increasingly important. The good news," the report added, "is that people are working longer, retiring later and in better health today than ever before."

The changing nature of retirement and work was also described by Neal Cutler, director of survey research at the National Council on Aging (NCOA) in Washington, D.C.

"We will see more and more people who describe themselves as retired, but continue to work," Cutler said. "Many of these people are working by choice, not because they have to. In the twenty-first century, retirement will encompass a wide range of options. We will see some 75-year-olds working two jobs and some 40-year-olds lounging poolside.

"Retirement," Cutler continued, "used to be defined by what one was no longer doing—not parenting, not working, not actively involved. Increasingly it will be defined by what one does do—second career, volunteer work, travel, sports activities."

Cutler's comments accompanied the findings of a national survey taken by Harris Interactive, Inc., for NCOA and the International Longevity Center. The survey showed that most Americans no longer think you've reached old age simply because you've turned 60 or 65 or 70.

Only 14 percent of those surveyed said reaching a specific age indicates that you are old. By contrast, 41 percent said that a decline in physical ability meant you were getting old. And 32 percent said that a decline in mental ability was an indicator of old age.

As chronological age becomes less of a factor in retirement thinking, good health becomes more of a factor in keeping retirees active. Among those surveyed who responded that they were retired, 15 percent said they continued to work full time, while 35 percent said they did volunteer work. That means that half of American retirees are not spending their time turning into couch potatoes. Unfortunately, the survey doesn't tell us what the other half are doing.

In my case, eight months after I retired I went back to work part time, writing a column on retirement and writing freelance articles.

I was fortunate. The column acted as a bridge between my full-time, 100-miles-an-hour working life and what could have been a zero-miles-an-hour retirement. Writing columns for *The Washington Post* helped me ease into retirement gradually.

Better yet, it allowed me to stay in touch with my colleagues at the newspaper. I am happy to go to the office occasionally to pick up mail, chat with old friends, or go to lunch with business contacts. For me, it's the best of both worlds.

Retiring with your spouse: The togetherness test

When you start to weigh the pros and cons of whether to retire, take a few minutes to think about what life will be like for you after you leave your job—especially if you are married.

When my wife, Sara, and I retired from the business world, one of the questions we faced was "What will it be like to stay at home and spend 24 hours a day with each other?"

Although we had been married for more than 40 years, we had no idea what the answer would be. In all those years, we had never been home together full time. After our marriage, Sara spent 18 years at home raising our three children. Then she went to work at GE.

We both held busy, demanding jobs. Sara worked an early shift and I worked a late shift, so we didn't see each other on weekdays for more than a few hours. On weekends, our time was taken up with chores, family activities, or social engagements. In short, there wasn't much time to be bored. If we had a quarrel, we could go to our respective offices the next day and cool off.

Our way of life changed dramatically when Sara retired from GE and I retired from the *Post*. Gone were the established routines of office life and the constant demands of our jobs. We enjoyed a new sense of freedom, but it was accompanied by a feeling that we weren't exactly the same people any longer—that we'd lost our purpose in life.

After several years, I can report that our concerns about full-time togetherness have faded and we've adjusted reasonably well to our new lifestyle. How were we able to do that? There were two main reasons:

1. *Sara and I did not go through the "turf battle" that causes problems for many retired couples.* A turf battle can arise when a woman, who views the home as her domain, finds that her

retired husband is underfoot all day and interferes with her routine. She may feel that her territory has been invaded. He may feel that he is unwelcome in his own home—and is unable to understand why.

A glimpse of the problem can be seen in the old joke about the wife who says to her newly retired husband, "Just remember, I married you for better or for worse. But not for lunch."

Sara and I avoided a turf battle in part because she had a long career at GE. So while she did not escape the daily household chores that fall to most working women, she had not been a full-time homemaker for two decades before retirement.

In addition, we sold our house shortly before we retired and moved to an apartment. The effect was to create a new domain where neither of us had any territorial claims.

2. *Sara and I organized our lives so we had time alone and time together.* Sara retired first. By the time I retired 2½ years later, she'd already developed a schedule of social and community activities that kept her busy on Mondays, Tuesdays, and Wednesdays.

I quickly realized that Sara's schedule was an opportunity for me to get both the "space" and the time that I needed. On the days she is busy, I work on my freelance writing, take care of family paperwork, exercise at the community fitness room, have lunch with friends, or play golf.

So, for part of the week, we each have our own schedules. In time, with Sara's help, I began to understand the need that women have for the companionship of other women. Sara explained that her games, lunches, and shopping trips all help fill that need.

"I like to spend time with my women friends and talk about the things women are interested in," Sara told me.

Living in a retirement community, I've also observed that retired men don't make new friends with other men as easily as retired women make new friends with other women. Several men have told me that they miss their male colleagues at the office and all the chatter about football, baseball, basketball, etc. That's one of the things I missed about my office.

Recognizing that fact, I joined the Lions, an international service organization. Our local club is mostly male, which gives me an opportunity to meet and spend time with other men my age.

On Thursdays, Fridays, Saturdays, and Sundays, Sara and I do things together: We might go to a new Smithsonian museum exhibition in Washington, D.C., take a day trip with friends to the eastern shore of Maryland, or just visit a shopping mall. I prefer museums to malls; Sara prefers malls. We keep the peace by taking turns.

Since we retired, we've also solved the weekly food-shopping problem. We do it together. For years, Sara did almost all the food shopping, often after a long day's work. Now that I'm retired, I don't think she should lug all those grocery bags herself. After all, I'm the one who's lifting weights every day.

In the beginning, our shopping experiences were quite tense. We had different priorities about what to buy and different recollections of what food items were still in the cupboard or refrigerator. Apparently, we were not alone, because we'd frequently hear couples arguing in the aisles about what to buy or not to buy.

We both hated that scene. So I promised myself that when Sara picked an item off the shelf, I would stop saying, "Do we really need that?" Ever since then, our shopping excursions became more relaxed.

On evenings when we eat at home, Sara and I get through dinner by using a team approach. She cooks and I clean up. The system has a double benefit. The meal is always excellent because of Sara's culinary skills, and that makes me happy. And Sara doesn't have to deal with the mess, which makes her happy.

This is the kind of partnership married people should strive for at all stages of their lives. But it's especially important when they're both retired.

Sara believes that if a couple wants to be happy in retirement, they need to be even more compatible than they were before they retired.

"When you retire, you'd better be friends," Sara says, "because you're going to be spending a lot of time together."

DECISION 2

Can I afford to retire?

Now that you've decided that you're ready to retire—or at least decided that you're ready to think about it seriously—let's talk about whether you can afford to retire.

On the face of it, the arithmetic of retirement is fairly simple. It's a matter of income versus expenses. The key question is, Will your monthly income be sufficient to cover your monthly expenses?

To get started, take a sheet of paper. On one side, list all the items of monthly income that you expect to receive when you retire. Add them up. On the other side of the paper, list all your monthly expenses and add them up. Then compare the numbers to see whether you have enough income to cover your expenses.

If you do have enough income, you're off to a good start. If you don't, you have to go to the next step where you have two basic choices: You can raise your income or lower your expenses. Either, as I learned from personal experience, is easier said than done.

However, there is another choice: Use your savings to help close the gap between income and expenses. Using your savings is a perfectly reasonable idea. After all, that's why you saved that money in the first place. But you must plan your withdrawals carefully; you don't want to dig into your savings too often or too deeply. Your nest egg may have to help support you for 15 or 20 years. In Chapter 7, we'll discuss how you can use your savings to provide a flow of monthly income.

A change in financial situation

One of the things that surprised me about retirement was the dramatic way in which my financial situation suddenly changed. One day I was receiving a sizable paycheck. The next day, it seemed, my paychecks had stopped. Intellectually, I was aware that my paychecks would stop when I retired. But I guess I wasn't fully prepared for the emotional jolt of losing that life-long security blanket.

In fact, there were several other major differences between working and retirement that I hadn't anticipated. Here are some of them:

Hello, fixed income

As full-time retirees, Sara and I are now living on a fixed income consisting mainly of our monthly Social Security benefits and our pension checks. We are fortunate to have pension checks. These days, many people do not receive pensions when they retire. But even if you get both Social Security benefits and a pension check, they are not likely to increase much over time. Social Security gives its beneficiaries an annual cost-of-living adjustment, which is usually quite modest. Most pensions are not adjusted for increases in the cost of living.

Goodbye, raises

When we were employed full time, our salaries were subject to occasional improvement. We were eligible for raises and promotions, both of which boosted our incomes. We were able to work overtime, which also increased our take-home pay. And, occasionally, we received bonuses. In short, there was a reasonable chance that we could increase the amount of money we made each year. But as retirees, we don't have those opportunities.

That means that the raises, overtime, and bonuses that helped pay for our new cars and summer vacations are not available in our retirement years. We'll have to find other ways to pay for large-ticket purchases or trips.

Health-care costs

Health costs in retirement are likely to be higher than they were while the person was employed. While Sara and I were working, we both had company health insurance, which covered medical, dental, and prescription bills. When we retired, we lost our company insurance.

Fortunately, we were both over 65 and thus were eligible to receive Medicare benefits. However, had we retired at age 62—an age when many people do retire—we could have been without health insurance for several years. The alternative would have been to buy private insurance until we were old enough to go on Medicare. That insurance would have been quite costly—and would have made a rather large hole in our retirement budget.

Neither of our employers had retiree health insurance plans available for us, so we signed up for Medicare, a national program that pays hospital and medical bills for 34 million people. In fairness to our former employers, *The Washington Post* provides retirees with an annual cash stipend, which can be used to buy a secondary insurance policy. The *Post* also allows retirees to buy low-cost catastrophic medical insurance coverage.

General Electric, for its part, provides its retirees with a secondary insurance policy that costs $130 a month for the two of us—a relative bargain. Equally important, GE allows its retirees and their spouses to join a prescription benefit plan that provides a 90-day supply of a medication for $20.

When you begin working on your retirement budget, don't forget that you probably will have to buy a secondary insurance or medigap policy to cover some of the expenses Medicare does not. I'll discuss medigap policies and their cost in Chapter 8. You may have to pay for your prescription drugs as well, which Medicare also does not cover. Prescriptions are covered by a few medigap policies, but those benefits may be limited.

The bottom line is that Sara and I are spending more money on our health care in retirement than we did while we were working and had company coverage—even though we paid for our company coverage.

Medicare, by the way, does not even pretend to cover all hospital or medical costs. Our GE secondary insurance plan covers some of the bills that Medicare does not pay. But even so, our annual out-of-pocket expenses for health care are perhaps 50 percent higher than when we were working.

We also worry—as we get older—whether we will encounter new medical problems and thus face even higher costs in the years ahead. Medical costs can be real budget busters.

When you are thinking about how much health-care money to include in your retirement budget, you may want to consider the cost of a long-term-care policy. For a 65-year-old, these policies can cost from $1000 to $3000 per year, depending on the terms of the policy. Sara and I are covered by a group policy we bought through *The Washington Post*. It costs $2000 a year for both of us—which is relatively inexpensive. I'll discuss long-term-care policies in Chapter 9.

The taxman cometh

In your retirement budget, you may need a special reserve for the money you owe for federal and state income taxes. During the years I worked, my employer always withheld money from my paycheck for income taxes. Usually, the amount of my withholding would be close to the actual amount of money I owed Uncle Sam at tax time. So it was easy to settle up with the IRS.

When I retired, I neglected to ask the *Post* to put tax withholding on my pension check. My Social Security check also did not have withholding. Sara and I later asked for withholding to be put on our pension checks, but we have not gotten around to putting withholding on our Social Security checks. [To do that, fill out IRS Form W-4V (*Voluntary Withholding Request*), and submit it to your local Social Security office.]

Initially, the effect of not having withholding on our Social Security and pension checks was that I had to file quarterly estimated income tax reports with the IRS and my state tax office. It also meant that I had to put aside a certain amount of money each month to cover the quarterly payments. I wasn't used to doing that, and it played havoc with my efforts to balance my family budget.

And, here is something else you should be aware of when it comes to taxes in retirement: Your Social Security payments may be taxable. Ignoring the fact that you paid taxes on the money you put into Social Security for many, many years, Uncle Sam will tax up to 80 percent of your Social Security benefits, depending on your taxable income.

Indeed, it is a good idea to talk to an accountant before retiring, to find out what your tax situation will be when you retire and what effect those taxes will have on the amount of money you'll have available to pay for your living expenses.

More about the taxman

As I will explain in Chapters 5 and 6, the beauty of the 401(k) plan is that it permits you to save money in a tax-deferred account for many years while you are working. It can reward you by producing a sizable retirement nest egg. But when you reach the magic age of 70½ years, Uncle Sam says you have to start withdrawing money from that account and paying taxes on your withdrawals.

As you prepare your retirement budget, especially if you are nearing 70½, remember that every dollar you withdraw from a tax-deferred IRA will be taxable. If, for instance, your taxable income is $40,000 and you take a $10,000 IRA withdrawal, your taxable income will become $50,000, and you will be taxed accordingly. So here again, you may need to set aside money in your budget for taxes—money you'd probably like to spend on other things.

Paying for your lifestyle

As you prepare to retire, you will hear a great deal of discussion about how much of your working income you will need in retirement to maintain the same lifestyle. You will hear financial advisors and others suggest that you will need about 80 percent of your regular income when you retire. That figure seems to assume that your living expenses as a retiree will be lower than they were when you were working full time. Well, maybe yes and maybe no.

The 80 percent rule hasn't worked for us. If anything, our living costs in retirement are higher than they were when we were both working. It makes sense if you think about it this way: When we retired, we did not relocate to a less expensive community, as did some of our friends. We stayed in the apartment that we moved into a few years before we retired. So our mortgage and condo fees have remained about the same. Our food bills also are about the same—although I don't understand why, since we're both dieting most of the time. It's true that we eat more restaurant meals than we used to—probably because we're home more and have more free time.

As for clothing, I haven't bought a new suit in some time—I don't need them much for business anymore—but there's been an increase in the amount of casual clothing that Sara and I have bought in recent years.

Moreover, we still drive two cars. Sara and I have talked about going to one car to save on the cost of insurance, gasoline, and repairs. But we both concluded that it wouldn't work. We are always going in different directions, and we just need the freedom that two cars provide.

Yes, we do save some money because we're not commuting to work every day—but not that much. We probably use the same number of gallons of gas visiting our local shopping malls.

Other expenses, such as our electric and telephone bills, have either remained the same or gone up. For instance, Sara and I both have cell phones for highway emergencies and the convenience of being able to stay in touch. But that's $50 a month that we did not spend a couple of years ago.

Our budget also has changed when it comes to entertainment. Going out to dinner with friends is the number-one leisure-time activity in our part of the country. We also subscribe to several local theater groups and regularly attend their shows, something we didn't have time for when we were working. In addition, we go to the John F. Kennedy Center for the Performing Arts in Washington, D.C. when community groups organize theater parties and bus transportation. The usual price is $50 or $60 a ticket.

Our retirement savings, I confess, took a big hit when we began to travel after we retired. We had both worked for many, many years and felt that we were entitled to enjoy some of the pleasures that go with retirement. So we took several cruises. Our cruise to Scandinavia and Russia was memorable, but the cost of our trip was about $15,000, in part because it included a week of sightseeing in London.

My point is that when you are planning your retirement, it is foolhardy to think that you will be happy living like a pauper. You don't live that way now while you are working, and there's no reason to plan to live that way when you retire.

At the very least, make sure that your income and your expenses—adjusted for the factors I have mentioned—allow you to have the kind of lifestyle to which you have become accustomed. Remember, too, that you will want to have some fun in retirement. But the cost of fun will be extra.

If your arithmetic shows that you can keep your lifestyle and also have some fun, then you can afford to retire. But if your retirement numbers show that you can't make ends meet, even by judicious withdrawals from savings, then you may have to delay your retirement and keep working until your finances improve.

Continuing to work past 65, for instance, can improve your retirement income in two ways: First, Social Security provides a bonus for every year you work past the normal retirement age up to age 70. The normal age for retirement is moving up gradually from 65 to 66 and will rise to 67 in the future. If you retired in 2000 at age 70, you would have gotten five years of delayed retirement credit and a bonus of 22.5 percent. Thus, a $1000 monthly Social Security check would have turned into about $1225.

Second, if you are entitled to a pension from your company and you continue to work, your pension may improve because of your additional earnings and because of pay raises. If your retirement budget looks like it could be tight, find out how much money you will receive both from Social Security and from your company pension if you work until age 70—assuming that your company will let you work until that age.

I retired at the age of 69 and found that both my Social Security and my pension were considerably higher than if I had retired at 65. Waiting to retire turned out to be a big help financially.

The power of time

When I step back and look at the list of items I have just discussed—the items that can seriously affect one's retirement budget—it is hard not to wish that I had saved more money during my working years. Indeed, I often wish that I had been wiser or more farsighted in building my retirement nest egg.

I'm not complaining. We did not save as much as some of our friends. But we saved more than other friends. So we're somewhere in the middle. And while we're reasonably secure financially, we still have to worry about whether we could run out of money during our retirement.

Perhaps if we had started saving earlier, we wouldn't have to worry about that. In recent years, I've learned that what you do about your money when you are 30, 40, or 50 will determine whether you can retire comfortably at 60, 65, or 70.

Ideally, the wise or foresighted individual will begin to save regularly at age 30, putting aside as much money as he or she can, month after month and year after year, for 30 or 35 years. Then, if the financial markets do what they have done for the last 50 years, the saver will reach retirement age with a sizable pot of money—enough to pay for a comfortable retirement, even if it lasts for 20 or 25 years. As I say, that's the ideal scenario.

My own experience was far from ideal. As a young reporter, I was married and had three children, a small house, a big mortgage, and a salary on which I could barely make ends meet. My wife was a stay-at-home mom, so we had to manage on my modest newspaper salary. Saving money was a near impossibility.

In the 1950s, the 401(k) plan had not yet been invented, and U.S. savings bonds were the most common vehicles of the day for saving money, except perhaps for the Christmas Club at the local bank. In any event, I was like most young people. For me, retirement was a word with little meaning. When I turned 40 in 1967, people were "old" at 65 and were thought to be lucky if they reached the biblical goal of "three score and ten," or 70.

The concept of a long, healthy retirement that took people into their eighties and nineties had not yet emerged. It was not until the 1980s, and especially the 1990s, that saving for retirement became a national mantra, aided by the aging of the nation's 77 million baby boomers, the growth of the 401(k) plan, and the hype of the $7 trillion mutual fund industry.

Looking back to when I was 40, I can see why it's so hard to talk to people in their thirties and forties about retirement and to convince them to save for their futures. The first problem, of course, is that when you're that age, retirement seems just too far away to worry about. The second problem is that when you're that age, there's a good chance that your monthly bills are going to eat up every penny you bring home.

Basically, that's what happened to me. It wasn't until I was 50 or 55 years old, after my children were grown and out on their own, after my salary had improved, and after my wife returned to work, that we got a chance to do some serious saving.

While that was the good news, the bad news was that we had wasted many years that could have helped us achieve our retirement savings goals. And that was a shame, because, in the battle for financial survival, the best weapon is time itself. I believe sincerely that when it comes to building your nest egg, it is almost as great a sin to waste time as it is to waste money.

Time can turn a modest amount of regular savings into a hefty amount of money. If you invest $100 a month for 15 years at a rate of 6 percent, you will wind up with $29,082. On the other hand, if you invest $100 a month at the same interest rate for 30 years, you will wind up with $100,452, more than three times as much.

The number of dollars you put into an investment is important, of course. But this example shows that the amount of time you give an investment is equally important. Why? Because money makes money.

People in the financial community often tell a story that may or may not be factual, but makes an important point about saving. The story is that Albert Einstein, the eminent physicist, was once asked, "Professor, in your opinion, what is the greatest invention the world has ever known?" Einstein thought for a moment and then replied, "Compound interest!"

Now, compound interest sounds like a mysterious concept if you're not familiar with it. But it's not. Here's a simple example: Let's say you invest $100 at 6 percent interest a year and never add to it. In the first year, the $100 earns $6 in interest. You then have $106. In the second year, the $106 earns 6 percent, or $6.36, giving you a total of $112.36. In the third year, the account grows to $119.10 . . . and so on. If you let your $100 grow and compound over 20 years, you will wind up with $321. In other words, your money will more than triple in 20 years, even though you never added another dollar to your account.

The power of compound interest can be quite awesome, especially when given enough time.

How to make your money grow

Now that we can see how money grows, the next question is "What's the best way to make your money grow in those all-important years before retirement?" There are, to be sure, many choices. But some are particularly worthwhile, because they come equipped with tax breaks that Uncle Sam hopes will encourage you to save for retirement.

Saving at work

The most important savings program, in my view, is the 401(k) plan, which many companies offer to their employees. A fuller description of 401(k) plans is in Chapter 5, but here's a brief description of the plan and why you should join if it is available where you work.

Typically, the plan allows you to contribute a percentage of your salary each week or month to a savings account set up in your name. Let's say you put in 6 percent of your pay. Your employer may then match part of your contribution by putting in, say, 3 percent of your pay, for a total contribution of 9 percent.

The company's contribution is often called "free money," but the best part of getting a "company match" is that it increases the number of dollars you have working—and compounding—for you in your account. Professor Einstein would approve.

Many companies hire mutual fund firms to manage the money that goes into their 401(k) plans. In those cases, you and your fellow employees will be given a list of the mutual funds that are available to you. It will then be your responsibility to decide which fund or funds you want to invest your money in.

When it comes to saving, the 401(k) plan has some special advantages. One main advantage is that the money you contribute is deducted from your pay before federal income taxes are withheld. That reduces your income taxes, a welcome, if temporary, tax break. Eventually, you will have to make up for those unpaid taxes—but not until you start to take money out of your account, and that could be many years in the future. Indeed, you could wait until you are age 70½.

The other advantage to tax deferral is that it helps increase the number of dollars in your account that are available to multiply and grow.

The downside of the 401(k) plan is that eventually you have to pay taxes on your withdrawals. Most people feel that's a small price to pay for the privilege of being able to build a solid nest egg over a period of many years.

One question that I am frequently asked is "We have a 401(k) plan at work, but my employer doesn't match any of my savings. Should I join the plan and contribute anyway?" I would say, "Yes." It would be better to have the matching money, of course, but you still get a tax break when you put your money into the account, and it still can grow on a tax-deferred basis.

The Roth IRA

If you are putting as much money as you are allowed to into your 401(k) plan at work and have additional money available for investment, you might want to think about opening up a Roth IRA. The Roth IRA was named for Senator William V. Roth of Delaware, who is chairman of the Senate Finance Committee. Unlike IRAs, which give you a tax deduction when you open them, the Roth IRA does not. If you fall within certain income limits, you can invest up to $2000 a year in a Roth IRA.

To be eligible to open a full Roth IRA, a single person must have a modified adjusted gross income below $95,000 a year.

Married couples who file jointly must have an income below $150,000.

The beauty of a Roth IRA is that after you reach age 59½ and have owned the IRA for five years, you can take out the full amount without paying any taxes. Or, if you wish, you can keep the money invested without ever taking it out. Those two features can be a major advantage to a retiree.

The Roth IRA came along after I retired, so I did not have a chance to make use of it. But if it had been available when I was younger, I would have tried to fund one each year. Having Roth IRA money available would have been a major advantage after I retired.

While Sara and I were grateful for the money we saved in our 401(k) plans at work, every dollar we take out of those accounts is fully taxable. When I reached 70½, I had to start withdrawing money from those accounts, as I explain in Chapter 6.

The Roth IRA doesn't give you a tax break when you open the account. But it allows your money to grow tax free over many years. And since you can take it out tax free, that's a pretty good deal.

Tax-efficient funds

If, after fully funding your 401(k) plan at work and opening up a Roth IRA each year, you still have additional money available, you might consider investing in a "tax-efficient" mutual fund. These funds are aimed at reducing the amount of taxes that shareholders pay each year on distributions. The way they do that is by lowering or eliminating both the dividend income and capital gains that they would otherwise pass on to shareholders. These twin goals are achieved in several ways. First, tax-efficient funds reduce the amount of buying and selling in their portfolios, thereby minimizing capital gains. Second, they try to avoid capital gains taxes by offsetting gains with losses. Finally, they often invest in low- or no-dividend stocks that are likely to grow in market value, but that do not produce income.

Tax-efficient funds are of relatively recent vintage, but they are widely available, especially from major fund companies. Index funds, which have been around for a long time, are also considered tax-efficient, because there is relatively little turnover in their portfolios. Table 2.1 shows the impact of taxes on stock fund returns.

The table presents the three-year average annual returns through 1999 for nine categories of stock mutual funds, before and after taxes. The funds are categorized by market capitalization (large, medium, small) and investment style (value, blend, growth). Note that many of the returns shown are far above historical norms and are not necessarily indicative of future returns.

Tax-efficient funds are likely to grow in popularity in the coming years. Many baby boomers are accumulating large pools of retirement monies. As they move into higher tax brackets, they will be looking for ways to invest and reduce their taxes.

A comfortable retirement

A few years ago, I saw a sign in a Pennsylvania restaurant that said "Too old, too soon. Too wise, too late." I have never forgotten

Table 2.1   The Impact of Taxes on Stock Fund Returns

	Value (%)		Blend (%)		Growth (%)	
Large	Pretax:	14.7	Pretax:	22.6	Pretax:	31.4
	After tax:	12.0	After tax:	20.3	After tax:	28.5
Medium	Pretax:	10.7	Pretax:	16.5	Pretax:	28.6
	After tax:	7.9	After tax:	14.0	After tax:	25.4
Small	Pretax:	7.3	Pretax:	13.7	Pretax:	24.9
	After tax:	5.7	After tax:	11.8	After tax:	22.8

Sources: Morningstar, Inc. The Vanguard Group.

that bit of wisdom, because it seemed to summarize my regrets about not paying closer attention to my personal finances when I was younger. It now seems perfectly obvious that I should have saved more aggressively during my working years. Social Security and pensions are helpful, but it is our savings that will make it possible for us to have a comfortable retirement. So save as much as you can. And when you finally sit down to draw up your retirement budget, your income will outweigh your expenses, and you'll be able to say, "Yes. I can afford to retire."

For more information

BOOKS

Bledsoe, John D. *Roth to Riches. The Ordinary to Roth IRA Handbook.* Legacy Press, Dallas, TX, 1998.

Trock, G. R. *The Roth IRA Made Simple: Pay No Taxes at Retirement.* Conquest Publishing, Inc., Griffith, IN, 1998.

WEB SITES

Roth IRA Web site: www.rothira.com. Provides technical, planning, and current news information on Roth IRAs to practitioners and consumers.

T. Rowe Price Associates: www.troweprice.com. Offers retirement planning software that can be downloaded or purchased by mail.

Vanguard Group: www.vanguard.com. Offers a Roth conversion worksheet that helps you determine whether it makes sense to convert your existing IRA assets to a Roth IRA.

When should I apply for Social Security?

Life is full of milestones. There are graduations and weddings, birthdays and anniversaries, and many more memorable events. Retirement is one of those milestones. I remember the day I picked up the telephone, dialed 1-800-772-1213, and told a representative of the Social Security Administration (SSA) that I was ready to apply for retirement benefits.

Several years have passed since I made that phone call, but I can clearly recall that I was nervous as I notified the U.S. government that at the age of 69, I had decided to retire. I guess I was nervous because making that call was akin to saying, "OK, pal, this is it. Your retirement is official. There's no going back."

After that, it took me a while to realize how quickly the phone call to the SSA changed my status in life. At one moment I was an active, hardworking member of the American workforce, with a paycheck coming in regularly. At the next moment, I was a retired person, who would henceforth depend on Social Security benefits to help me pay for my living expenses.

I wasn't entirely comfortable with the idea of being so dependent on Social Security. But it was exhilarating to think that after 50 years of contributing to the system, I was finally going to get something back. At that point, I wasn't sure how much I would get each month, but I knew that it would be an important part of my retirement income. I was also comforted to know that the payments would continue for the rest of my life.

In fact, it was only after Sara and I decided to retire—and applied for our benefits—that we began to learn how Social Security works. Fortunately, we had not needed any of the agency's support services earlier in our lives. But that meant that we had no occasion to learn about the workings of its many benefit programs.

I realize now that I arrived at retirement age with little knowledge of the role Social Security plays in our national life. Nor did I understand the value of the safety net that the SSA provides for millions of elderly and disabled Americans and for families that have lost their breadwinners.

Like many Americans, I tended to think of Social Security as a savings bank. I thought that the payroll taxes taken out of my salary each payday would be deposited in Washington, earn interest, and eventually be returned to me when I retired. I could not have been more wrong, for that is not the way the system works.

Social Security, I discovered, is not a bank at all. It is, essentially, a national social insurance program that uses the taxes paid by American workers and their employers to create a giant pool of money. It's a pay-as-you-go system, in the sense that the money that goes into the pool is then paid out to people eligible for benefits. Indeed, one of the main concerns about the future of Social Security is that we will reach a time when there will be far fewer people putting money into the pool than are taking money out.

The key goal of Social Security is to provide a minimum income—sometimes called a "floor of protection"—for workers and their families. Among these individuals are people who reach retirement age, workers who become disabled, and families that lose their wage earners. An estimated 96 percent of all American workers contribute to the system.

Kenneth S. Apfel, the commissioner of Social Security, frequently stresses the value of the income protection that his agency gives to disabled persons and surviving family members. For an average wage earner with a spouse and two children, Apfel says, the disability benefits are equal to a $233,000 disability policy. At the same time, he says, the income protection given to survivors of a deceased worker is equal to a $354,000 life insurance policy.

"Social Security is more than a retirement program," Apfel says. And his agency's figures show that to be true. In 1999, about 45 million Americans received almost $385 billion in benefits. Here's how the $385 billion were shared:

- Seventy percent of the benefits went to 31 million retired workers and their dependents. The average monthly benefit was $804.

- Fourteen percent went to 6.5 million disabled workers and their dependents. The average monthly benefit was $754.
- Sixteen percent went to 7 million survivors of deceased workers. The average monthly payment was $774.

The importance of the safety net becomes even more apparent when you dig into those figures and find that

- Two thirds of aged beneficiaries get 50 percent or more of their income from Social Security.
- Social Security is the only source of income for about 18 percent of the elderly. Without Social Security, 50 percent of the elderly would be living in poverty. (The poverty rate for elderly Americans dropped from 35 percent in 1959 to 11 percent in 1997.)

What are your benefits based on?

When it comes time to pay benefits to retirees, how does the agency decide who gets what? It's a question I never thought about, and I doubt whether many other people have done so either. The fact is that there is a specific social philosophy that determines the payment of benefits, and this philosophy has several components. For instance, the formulas are designed so that there is a clear link between what you pay into the system during your working years and the benefits you receive when you retire. People who earn high wages during their careers generally will get higher benefits than people who earn low wages.

However, one key feature of the payment philosophy tends to level the playing field: The formula used to compute benefits includes factors which ensure that lower paid workers get a higher return than highly paid workers. Social Security's progressive benefit structure helps compensate for the fact that low-wage earners have less opportunity to save and invest.

Low-wage earners retiring at 65 in January 2000 had about 56 percent of their preretirement income replaced by Social Security; high-wage earners had about 28 percent of their preretirement income replaced by Social Security.

This idea of paying out benefits according to the relative needs of individuals and their families carries through when the agency deals with the disabled and with families that experience the death of their primary wage earner. For instance, a disabled worker with a family to support will draw higher benefits than a disabled worker with no dependent family.

Inevitably, some people get far less in Social Security benefits than they contributed. Others get far more. A worker who contributes to Social Security for 30 years, but dies before he or she can retire, gets no retirement benefit. On the other hand, a widow with two young children, whose husband dies at age 35, will draw benefits for many years, even though her husband contributed relatively little money to the system.

Looking back, I wish I had learned about Social Security long before I retired. The agency offers future retirees several retirement options that I did not know about, each with its own advantages and disadvantages. In the end, I might have retired exactly when I did, but it would have been wise to learn about my options in advance.

As I said earlier, I retired at the age of 69. I draw a Social Security benefit of about $1600 a month—thanks to a lifetime of steady work, salary increases, and a blind love of the newspaper business that kept me working for four years past the normal retirement age of 65.

Sara, who worked for GE for 22 years, draws a Social Security benefit of $1000. We're grateful for both payments, which are an important part of our retirement income.

But as we discovered—somewhat too late, perhaps—the time to start thinking about retiring on Social Security is when you are in your fifties or early sixties.

Your first opportunity to retire and receive Social Security benefits comes at age 62. After that, you can retire at any age, although most people retire by the time they are 70. The choice is yours. But there are several things you should know, because they may affect the timing of your decision.

However, before we discuss retirement options, let's take a small detour to discuss several major changes that are taking place in Social Security's retirement benefits.

Raising the retirement age

For as long as anyone can remember, age 65 has been the "normal" retirement age. The SSA calls age 65 the "full retirement age," meaning that at age 65 you become eligible to receive your full retirement benefits.

But all that is changing. In 1983, Congress decided to raise the full retirement age from 65 to 67. The change was part of a sweeping measure that strengthened Social Security's finances by generating an additional $165 billion for the system.

The 1983 package not only boosted the retirement age; it also boosted payroll tax rates for workers, employers, and the self-employed; it delayed cost-of-living adjustments and levied taxes on benefits received by some high-wage earners. The SSA estimates that between 2000 and 2009 alone, the continuing increase in the retirement age will save the federal government $22.1 billion.

Table 3.1 shows the age one must reach to qualify for full Social Security benefits. The upward move from age 65 to age 67, as shown in the table, will begin in 2003 and will affect persons born in 1938. In 2003, an individual born in 1938 who wants to retire will have to be age 65 and two months in order to qualify for full retirement benefits. After that, the age for receiving full benefits will continue to climb gradually, reaching

TABLE 3–1 Full Retirement Age Goes from 65 to 66. . .to 67

Year of Birth	Full Retirement Age
1937 or earlier	65
1938	65 and 2 months
1939	65 and 4 months
1940	65 and 6 months
1941	65 and 8 months
1942	65 and 10 months
1943–1954	66
1955	66 and 2 months
1956	66 and 4 months
1957	66 and 6 months
1958	66 and 8 months
1959	66 and 10 months
1960 and later	67

Note: Persons will still be able to take their retirement benefits at age 62, but the payments will be reduced.

Source: Social Security Administration.

66 in 2009 and rising to age 67 over a 22-year period. However, for 11 of those interim years, between 2009 and 2020, the retirement age will remain at 66. It will then resume its upward path, reaching 67 in 2027.

In deciding to increase the retirement age, Congress cited improvements in the health of older people and dramatic increases in life expectancy. Today, at age 65, men can expect to live until almost 81. At age 65, women can look forward to living until 84.

Although 2003 will be the first year in which people will have to be somewhat older than 65 to retire with full benefits, the impact of the age change was felt for the first time in 2000 by people who retired at age 62. This is how they were affected and how the early-retirement option is changing:

Your retirement options

Option one: early retirement

Even though the retirement age is rising to 67, you will still be able to retire at age 62 if you are willing to take a permanently reduced Social Security payment. The idea behind the reduction is this: Because you are likely to be drawing benefits for a longer period of time, you get less money per month at age 62 than if you retired at 65.

How much is the reduction? Until 2000, if you retired at 62, you got 80 percent of your benefits, a reduction of 20 percent. However, as the retirement age rises from 65 to 67, the deduction for early retirement at 62 will increase gradually to 30 percent. For instance, if your full retirement age is 65 and two months and you retired at 62 in 2000, you got only 79.17 percent of your benefits, a reduction of 20.83 percent. If your full retirement age is 65 and four months and you retire at 62 in 2001, you get 78.33 percent of your full benefits, a reduction of 21.67 percent. The reduction will increase slowly until it reaches 30 percent for people who retire at age 62 in 2022.

Here's a retirement warning: If you are a married man who is thinking about retiring at 62, you may want to consider the impact that early retirement could have on your spouse. Here is an example:

John Q. Worker retires at 62 and takes a reduced Social Security payment of $800 a month. That figure represents a 20 percent reduction from the $1000 a month he would have gotten if he retired at 65. His spouse, Mary Q. Worker, also retires at 62 and gets a benefit of $600 a month.

When John is 70, he dies. Mary is entitled to receive her husband's $800 a month payment instead of her $600 payment, because his is more than hers.

However, while Mary will get $800, it is far less than the $1400 they were receiving together. If John had waited until he was 65 to retire, he would have gotten $1000 a month. On his death, Mary also would get $1000 a month.

Because women tend to outlive men, that's a scenario that is worth thinking about before you make your decision about when to retire.

Option two: normal retirement

You can retire at 65 or at whatever age you become eligible for full retirement benefits. At this writing, the age is still 65, but starting in 2003, the age for full benefits will begin creeping up, from 65 to 66 and then to 67.

One key question to consider before taking your benefits when you reach your full retirement age is: Do you want to delay retirement to increase your monthly Social Security benefit? To answer this question, consider how the Social Security system works: Your retirement benefits are based on your earnings history and other factors. This means that you will get a specific amount of Social Security benefits over your lifetime if you live to an average age.

If you begin taking benefits early at 62, you will get more monthly payments, but with fewer dollars in each check. If you don't take your benefits until you are 70, you will get fewer monthly checks, but with more dollars in each check. In addition, those who work beyond 65 may get additional benefits because of their extra years of work.

Option three: late retirement

You can work past your full retirement, which increases your monthly benefits. For people who turn 65 in 2000 or in 2001, a special yearly credit of 6 percent will be added for each year they delay retirement. The bonus ends at age 70.

TABLE 3.2 Social Security Delayed Retirement Credits

Year of Birth	Yearly Rate of Increase (%)
1930	4.5
1931–1932	5.0
1933–1934	5.5
1935–1936	6.0
1937–1938	6.5
1939–1940	7.0
1941–1942	7.5
1943 or later	8.0

Source: Social Security Administration.

People who were born in either 1935 or 1936 and work until age 70 would get a 6 percent a year bonus for five years, or a total of 30 percent more than they would have gotten if they retired at 65. That bonus will rise 0.5 percent every two years in the future, reaching 8 percent for people born in 1943 and later.

The increases for delayed retirement are shown in Table 3.2. If you delay your retirement beyond your full retirement age, Social Security benefits will be increased by a certain percentage, depending on your date of birth. The increase in benefits stops when you reach age 70, even if you continue to delay taking benefits.

In 2027, when the full retirement age will be 67, people who work until age 70 will get only three years of bonus payments.

Which option is best?

After I retired, I began to wonder whether a retiree would collect more total dollars by retiring at 62, at 65, or at 70. It was not an easy thing to figure out, so I asked the SSA to do it for me.

Let's assume, I said, that we're talking about a person who was born in 1940, turned 60 in 2000, and is trying to decide, from a financial point of view, at what age it would be best to retire. Let's also assume that that the person earned $50,000 in 2000 and, starting at age 22, had steady lifetime earnings that increased each year at the national average. We also will assume that the person will live until age 80.

According to SSA actuaries, as shown in Table 3.3, this hypothetical person would receive the most total dollars by retiring at age 65: $366,492. If the person retired at 70, he or she would receive slightly less: $364,812. And if the person retired at 62, he or she would get a lot less: only $331,320. All those figures include annual cost-of-living adjustments (COLAs).

The folks at SSA are quick to point out that benefit amounts for real individuals could differ significantly from these estimates, depending on the worker's actual earnings and the actual cost-of-living adjustments. Also, since SSA bases your benefit, in part, on your average earnings over a 35-year period, your

TABLE 3.3   How Do You Earn the Most Social Security Benefits?

Individual Retiring January 2002 at Age 62 Years, 0 Months

Initial monthly benefit:	$1,166
Total benefits to age 80 (including annual COLAs)	$331,320

Individual Retiring January 2005 at Age 65 Years, 6 Months

Initial monthly benefit:	$1,654
Total benefits to age 80 (including annual COLAs)	$366,492

Individual Retiring January 2010 at Age 70 Years, 0 Months

Initial monthly benefit:	$2,616
Total benefits to age 80 (including annual COLAs)	$364,812

Source: Social Security Administration.

monthly payment could go up if your peak earning years were to occur between ages 65 and 70. In any event, the total amount of benefits you receive will depend on how long you live.

As the table shows, the monthly benefit that our hypothetical person would receive goes up the later the individual retires. At 62, the payment is $1166; at 65, it is $1654, and at 70, it is $2616. That could be a significant factor for people who need the biggest possible Social Security payment to help make ends meet when they retire. Thus, if your job is secure, your health is good, and you can continue to work until you are 70, it may be worthwhile to wait to get a larger check at 70, rather than a smaller check at 65.

After looking at these figures, I began to wonder what people actually do when it comes to choosing a time to retire. It turns out, the SSA tells me, that 59 percent of people who retire on Social Security do so at age 62, while another 20 percent retire at age 65, for a total of 79 percent. The other 21 percent take their benefits after 65.

Who pays for Social Security benefits?

We all do. Employers and employees pay equal amounts toward Social Security and Medicare. The tax rate in 2000 was 7.65 percent for employers and the same for employees. Of that amount, 6.2 percent was used to finance Social Security retirement, disability, and survivors' benefits, and 1.45 percent went toward the Medicare program. In 2000, employers withheld 7.65 percent of an employee's wages, up to $76,200. Employers paid a matching amount.

If an employee earned more than $76,200, the employer continued to withhold 1.45 percent of the rest of the worker's wages for Medicare The employer paid an equal amount.

Self-employed people pay both the employee's and employer's tax, a total of 15.3 percent. However, self-employed persons can deduct one half of that amount from their income for tax purposes.

As shown in Table 3.4, the amount of wages that can be taxed for Social Security contributions will continue to rise above the $76,200 level each year. By 2008, the maximum wages for Social Security levies are projected to be $100,800.

How do you qualify for Social Security?

If you were born in 1929 or later, you will need 40 credits to be eligible for retirement benefits. You earn your credits during your working years. Generally speaking, 40 credits represent 10 years of employment. Here's how eligibility is determined:

During your years of employment, your wages are posted on your Social Security record, and you earn credits based on those wages. The credits are used to determine your eligibility for retirement benefits or for disability or survivor benefits if you should become disabled or die.

In 2000, you received one credit for each $780 of earnings, up to a maximum of four credits per year. The SSA folks predict that,

TABLE 3.4 How Much of Your Income Will Be Taxed for Social Security?

Year	Up To
2001	$78,600
2002	$81,000
2003	$83,700
2004	$86,400
2005	$89,700
2006	$93,300
2007	$96,900
2008	$100,800

Source: Social Security Administration Projections.

in the future, it will take even more dollars to earn a credit than it does today, because of the steady national increase in average annual wages.

Note that when it comes to qualifying for retirement benefits, there are special rules for the self-employed, for people in the military, for farm and domestic workers, and for those who work for nonprofit organizations. There also are special rules for workers not covered by Social Security, as well as special guidelines for those claiming disability and survivor benefits. All this information can be found in SSA Publication 05-10072. Call 1-800-772-1213 for a copy of *Social Security: How You Earn Credits.*

How much will you get?

In October 1999, the SSA began sending out its newly designed Social Security statement to workers 25 or older who are not yet getting Social Security benefits. Statements should arrive in your mailbox each year about three months before your birthday. The statements contain a record of your earnings and estimates of your retirement and disability benefits. If you don't get a statement, call 1-800-772-1213.

What will the statement tell you? Quite a lot, actually. It will tell you when you will reach your full retirement age. It also will give you an estimate of your benefits at age 62, at full retirement age, and at 70. The age-62 estimate will include the reduction for early retirement; the age-70 estimate will include the credits given for delayed retirement.

What is your benefit based on? Basically, Social Security retirement benefits are based on the amount of money you earned during your lifetime—with an emphasis on the 35 years in which you earned the most. This information is fed into SSA computers and subjected to several formulas we discussed earlier. Eventually, the SSA arrives at your basic benefit, or primary insurance amount (PIA). The PIA is what the agency considers to be your full retirement amount. The new benefits statement should be of great help to people who are eager to know how much money they can expect to receive when they retire.

Conceivably, if this annual look ahead shows some individuals that their future benefits will be small, it could inspire these low-wage earners to increase their efforts to earn higher salaries in order to improve their chances of drawing higher retirement benefits.

Applying for Social Security benefits

There are two basic ways to apply for Social Security retirement benefits. One is to call the SSA and start the application process over the telephone. The other way is to ask for an appointment to go to your local Social Security office and apply in person.

Social Security's toll-free telephone number, 1-800-772-1213, operates 24 hours a day, including weekends and holidays. However, to apply for retirement or other benefits, you will need to speak to a representative. The phone reps are available from 7 A.M. to 7 P.M. on business days. People who are deaf or hard of hearing can call a toll-free "TTY" number, 1-800-325-0778.

When you call to apply for retirement benefits, the phone rep will schedule a telephone interview for you. At that time, you will be asked a number of questions and you will be requested to mail the originals of several important documents. When the documents are received by the SSA, they will be copied and returned to you.

If you would prefer to apply in person, the phone reps will make an appointment for you to visit your local SSA office. You also can use the toll-free line to inform the agency that you have changed your address or to arrange to send your monthly payment directly to your bank.

The information and documents you will need when you apply for retirement benefits generally include the following:

- Your Social Security number
- Your birth certificate
- Your W-2 forms or self-employment tax return for the previous year
- Your military discharge papers if you served in the armed forces
- Your spouse's birth certificate and Social Security number if he or she is applying for benefits
- Proof of U.S. citizenship or lawful alien status if you (or a spouse who is applying for benefits) were not born in the United States
- The name of your bank and your account number so that your benefits can be deposited directly into your account

The special-payments problem

Sometimes the best way to learn about a problem is to experience it. That's what happened to my wife and me. Sara retired in 1993, two and a half years before I did. As I recall, we each phoned the SSA and later visited our local office, bringing the required documents.

Dealing with the SSA was a relatively pleasant and low-key experience—at least until we ran into Sara's "special-payments" problem. That turned into a pretty confusing and nerve-wracking situation. Here's what happened:

Sara retired from General Electric on December 31, 1993, and began receiving Social Security benefits in February 1994. When Sara had applied for benefits several months earlier, she was asked what she expected to earn in 1994. Her answer was that she didn't expect to earn anything in 1994 because she was retiring and would not be working. However, when Sara retired, GE owed her $27,231 in severance pay and vacation pay, all related to her working years. Because she retired December 31, that money was paid to Sara early in 1994 and was reported on our income taxes for 1994.

In August 1995, Sara received a letter from the SSA saying, in effect: You told us that you would not earn any money in 1994. But now we see that you reported earnings of $27,231 that year. So, unless there are some things we don't know about, you have to give back $5,183 of your 1994 Social Security payments!

That letter sent Sara and me into overdrive, and after a flurry of phone calls and visits to our local SSA office, we finally discovered the problem: The agency did not know that the $27,231 represented severance and vacation pay that was due her for her work at GE before she retired.

That fact was important, because the SSA has a special set of rules that apply to those kinds of payments after you retire. Under these rules, Social Security does not count some types of "special payments" you receive after you leave your job—if the payments are related to services you provided to your company before you retired.

Sara was able to prove that she had not worked in 1994 by furnishing a letter from her employer, which showed that the $27,231 came from severance pay, vacation pay, and other monies owed. The SSA agreed that they were, indeed, "special payments," so Sara did not have to return any of her Social Security benefits.

While the situation was resolved to our satisfaction, it left us with a few more gray hairs than we had before. Several years later, when I retired from *The Washington Post* with my own severance and vacation pay package, I remembered Sara's experience. So I asked the newspaper to give me a letter showing what my payments covered. I filed the letter with Social Security and thus managed to head off a demand that I return a chunk of my Social Security benefits. When you retire, watch out for this one!

Running into the earnings limits

At first, Sara and I didn't understand why Social Security even cared about whether she earned any money after she retired. It took us a while to figure out that Sara had run into the Social Security "earnings limits." As it turned out, she didn't work in 1994 or earn any money in any manner, but the SSA initially assumed that she had worked and had gone over the earnings limit.

In the course of clearing up the confusion, we learned that if retirees work and go over the earnings limit, they have to give back some of their benefits. What we discovered was that there are two types of earnings limits. One applies to people who are between ages 62 and 64. The other applies to people between 65 and 69. At 70, you are free to earn as much as you want.

In 2000, Congress made a significant change in the earning limits. Here's the story:

At the start of 2000, if you were 65 to 69, you were scheduled to lose $1 in current benefits for every $3 you earned above $17,000. Thus, if you earned $20,000, you would have lost $1000 in current benefits. At least, that was the rule until April 2000, when Congress voted to repeal that part of the earnings limit, retroactive to January 1, 2000. President Clinton signed the bill April 7, 2000, with considerable fanfare.

However, the other half of the earnings limit remained intact. In 2000, if you were 62 to 64, you lost $1 in current Social Security payments for every $2 you earned over $10,080. Thus, if you earned $20,000, you lost $4960 in current benefits.

Normally, the earnings limits have been raised each year. That will continue to happen for the younger group of beneficiaries. For those who are 62 to 64 years old, the earnings limit is $11,280 in 2002. A different limit applies during the months before you reach your full retirement age—(now 65 but rising to age 67). Ask SSA for details.

Even so, Sara's run-in with those "special payments" could be experienced by anyone age 62 to 64 who retires and is given severance or vacation pay for service to the company while he or she was still working. In that case, get your company to give you a letter explaining the payments, and send the letter to the SSA. Meanwhile, it does not appear that the earnings limit for people in the 62-to-64 age group will be repealed anytime soon. There are 250,000 retirees in this group, and they lose an estimated $600 million a year in benefits.

While there was widespread support for repealing the limit on the 65-to-69 age group, similar support was lacking for repeal of the limit on the 62-to-64 age group. For instance, SSA Commissioner Apfel supported repeal for the older group in order to encourage older workers to stay in the labor force. However, he opposed repeal for the younger group because of the long-term impact on millions of elderly widows.

As I mention earlier in this chapter, people who retire at 62 have their retirement benefits permanently reduced by 20 percent to account for the fact that they will be receiving payments for a longer period of time. When married men retire at 62 and take reduced benefits, it can have a serious impact on their spouses.

Eventually, when these men die, their widows receive benefits that are even further reduced. Apfel said that repealing the earnings limits for the 62-to-64 age group would encourage more people to retire younger, and that, he believed, would cause a significant increase in poverty, especially for elderly widows.

Repeal of the earnings limit

The repeal of a major portion of the Social Security earnings limit was, as you might imagine, an occasion for many retirees to celebrate. The rule was extremely unpopular with retirees who wanted to work but did not like the idea of giving up part of their current benefits to do so. In fact, until the law's repeal, many of my fellow retirees had had a special reason to celebrate when they reached their seventieth birthdays: Turning 70 meant they could work and earn as much as they wanted. Now they can do so at age 65.

Until the law was partially repealed, about 900,000 beneficiaries between the ages of 65 and 69 gave up part or all of their current Social Security payments each year—a total of $6 billion—because they earned more than the law allowed. To avoid losing some of their Social Security payments, many retirees in America worked "up to the limit," each year, quitting when they earned the amount allowed.

Commissioner Apfel told me that he had had firsthand experience with the idea of working "up to the limit." The commissioner said that his father, Walter Apfel, a steel salesman, continued to work after he retired in his early sixties and began collecting Social Security benefits.

"When my father retired," Apfel said, "he would work right up to the earnings limit—and not work beyond it—because he did not want to lose his Social Security benefit." The commissioner said he tried to convince his father that even if he worked beyond the limit, he would not be truly losing his benefits in the long run. "I'd say to him, 'Dad, you're going to get it back. You lose it for that year, but it gets added on to your benefits for the rest of your life.'" The commissioner said his father was not convinced. "He'd say, 'I'm not sure what happens 10 or 15 years from now. I want to know what happens now.'"

One of the stumbling blocks to repealing the law was the initial cost of doing so. Partial repeal for the 65-to-69 age group was estimated to cost $20.4 billion over 10 years. Repeal for the younger group would have cost another $24.3 billion over 10 years. What finally made partial repeal happen was the growing budget surplus, a national labor shortage, and a fierce political battle for the votes of retirees and senior citizens in the year 2000. Advocates of repeal had argued that letting retirees work to their hearts' content would have beneficial economic and tax effects. They noted that retirees who keep working continue to contribute to Social Security and Medicare even though they are receiving retirement benefits. They also continue to pay income taxes.

The increase in the labor supply of people between 65 and 69 could translate into 63 million additional hours worked, or the equivalent of 31,500 more full-time jobs, according to a study by Aldona and Gary Robbins of the Institute for Policy Innovation, a conservative think tank in Lewisville, Texas. Further, the increase would boost the nation's gross domestic product, a measure of goods and services, by $19.5 billion and would add $6.8 billion to the nation's store of capital. "By 2010," the researchers said, "the extra revenue from added growth would be enough to offset the higher benefit payments that stem from eliminating the earnings limit."

One worker who rejoiced when Congress repealed the earnings limit was Antonio Santos, 68, a retired technician for Channel 4 in Dallas. Santos operates robotic cameras, a skill that is in heavy demand. Santos, who was unhappy with the earnings limit, said he tried to work fewer than 20 hours a week, but he wasn't always successful. In 1998, he recalled, he reached his earnings threshold by midyear and told his employer he would have to take the rest of the year off. However, when the TV station, where he worked for 45 years, desperately needed help, Santos said, he agreed to go in to work. That put him over the earnings limit. As a result, he had to give back part of his Social Security payments.

I talked to Santos on the day President Clinton signed the repeal bill. Santos was a happy man. "It's like a godsend for me. You can always use extra money when you're on a fixed retirement," he said. Being able to work part time is important to him because it means that he doesn't have to dig into his savings.

"I think that if a person is willing to work and is in good health, there should be no limit on what that person can earn," Santos said. There were many in Washington who agreed: The House and the Senate both passed the repeal bill unanimously.

Worrying about the future

When I retired and began to learn about Social Security, I had two main questions. First, How does Social Security work? In this chapter, I've tried to provide some basic answers to that question.

Second, Will Social Security still be around when my children and grandchildren retire? It would take a separate book to explore all the aspects of that question. Indeed, many such books have been written. But on the basis of what we know now, Social Security seems to be financially secure for the "short term," which covers the next three decades.

The 2000 report from the Social Security and Medicare boards of trustees tells us that the Social Security trust funds are "adequately financed" until 2037. This means that, until that year, there will be enough money coming into Social Security to pay 100 percent of the benefits due. After that, however, Social Security will begin to feel the effect of a shrinking workforce and a growing retiree force. As the years go on, fewer and fewer workers will be contributing to the system, while more and more workers will retire and stop contributing.

Today, there are 30 beneficiaries taking money out of the Social Security pool for every 100 workers putting money in. By 2010, the year that the baby boomers will begin to retire, there will be 33 beneficiaries receiving payments for every 100 workers. By 2034, that number will rise to 49 beneficiaries per 100 workers, and in 2075, it will go up to 54 beneficiaries per 100 workers.

Looking at the problem in another way, Figure 3.1 shows the decline in the number of workers for each Social Security beneficiary. From 3.7 workers in 1970, the number has dropped to 3.4 workers in 2000 and will drop sharply to 1.9 workers in 2075. These numbers offer a vivid demonstration of how rapidly America, the land of the free, is also becoming the home of the gray. Fortunately, 2037 is still far enough away to give Congress and the

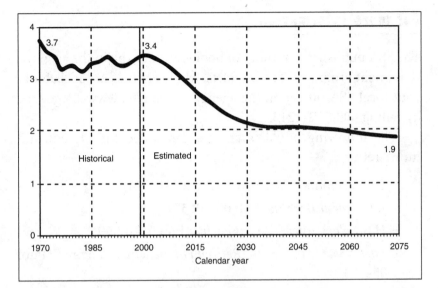

Figure 3.1   A look into the future. (Source: Social Security and Medicare Boards of Trustees 2000 Annual Reports.)

White House time to make the changes needed to shore up Social Security's future finances.

It's hard to forecast what the changes will be, although there is no shortage of ideas, plans, and schemes to reform and strengthen Social Security in the twenty-first century. But change will not come easily: When you try to change a program that affects 45 million Americans, you've got your work cut out for you.

For future retirees, the ongoing debate over Social Security will be both an opportunity and a challenge. I've already suggested that it's important to know how the system works, so you can make wise personal decisions about your retirement benefits. Now, let me suggest that it may be equally important for future retirees to take part in the national debate over how to save and improve the workings of the Social Security system. There's a great deal at stake in this debate for you, your children, and your grandchildren. All of us can, and should, help shape the future of Social Security.

For more information

The SSA publishes a number of booklets that explain the agency's retirement programs. The booklets, which are free, are available at your local SSA office; on the agency's Web site, www.ssa.gov; or by calling 800-772-1213.

The following booklets are recommended for present and future retirees:

- *Understanding the Benefits* (Pub.05-10024).
- *Retirement Benefits* (Pub.05-10035).
- *How Work Affects Your Benefits* (Pub.05-10069).
- *Fact Sheet: How Your Retirement Benefit Is Figured* (Pub. 05-10070).

DECISION 4

How should I take my pension payments?

Soon after I announced my retirement in the spring of 1996, I paid a visit to Michael C. Bahr, the benefits analyst in *The Washington Post*'s personnel department. For more than 20 years, Mike has shepherded hundreds of employees through the retirement process, helping them make crucial decisions on how to deal with both their pensions and their 401(k) savings plans. Mike always made time to answer my questions about *Post* benefits.

Over the years, Mike and I had often chatted about the ups and downs of the stock market and the mutual funds that were offered to employees who were part of the newspaper's 401(k) savings plan. But I do not recall that we ever spent much time talking about the inner workings of the *Post*'s pension plan.

For one thing, the likelihood that I'd retire someday always seemed to be rather remote. Second, I had a sense that pension plans were very complicated, and I had no desire to strain my brain with information I wouldn't need for quite a while. So, I never asked Mike to explain how the *Post* pension was calculated, although, looking back, I wish I had. It would have given me more time to think about my pension options before I retired.

Once a year, Mike sent *Post* employees a report that showed how much pension money each employee could expect to receive when he or she reached age 65. I recall that each year, as I looked at the figures in my report, I would think to myself, "That's not enough money to live on," and I would dismiss the idea of retiring.

Indeed, one of the reasons I worked until I was 69 was because I hoped that additional years on the job and a rising pay level would help improve my pension when I finally decided to take it. And that's exactly what happened.

Understanding your pension plan

There are, of course, two main types of pension plans: a defined benefit plan, which is paid for by the employer, and a defined contribution plan, such as a 401(k) savings plan, to which the employee, and often the employer, contribute.

The *Post*'s pension plan was a defined benefit plan. The *Post* paid all expenses; I put no money into it. The pension benefits I received were based on a formula that was, in turn, based on several factors, including the total number of years I worked at the paper, my average salary during my five highest paid years on the job, and the amount of money the company contributed to Social Security for me.

Using the *Post* formula, Mike figured out how much money I would get in my pension check each month if I took the maximum amount. He then told me I had several choices as to how I could take my monthly payments:

- A single life pension. This meant that I would receive my maximum pension of $2532 a month, before deductions. But I could draw that pension check only during my lifetime. When I died, the pension would cease and my wife would get nothing.
- A 50 percent spousal benefit. This meant that I could take a lower amount—about $2160 a month for as long as I lived. After my death, my wife would receive half of my check, or $1080 a month.
- A 100 percent spousal benefit. This meant that I would take an even lower benefit—about $1900 a month, but upon my death, my wife would receive the same $1900 check each month.

In other words, if I agreed to take less of a pension while I was alive, my spouse could continue to receive a pension check from the *Post* as long as she lived.

Making the pension decision

The question facing us was this: Was it better—from both a financial and a commonsense point of view—to take my full pension or to take either the 50 percent or 100 percent spousal benefit? At the time I retired, Sara was already retired. And we were concerned that it might be difficult for us to go from living on two full salaries to living on a combination of pensions and Social Security income. Understandably, we felt that we would like to go into retirement with as much monthly income as possible.

This wasn't just a matter of greed. As I noted in an earlier chapter, I hadn't given much thought to my retirement budget. And it didn't look like our monthly living expenses would go down much when we retired. In fact, it seemed like they might go up. In short, because we hadn't planned carefully for our retirement budget, it seemed like we would need all the income we could get.

There were other factors, too. Sara, who had retired about two years earlier, was getting a pension of about $700 a month from GE. I also had about $150,000 in life insurance. Our idea was that, if I died, Sara could invest the insurance money and, even at a low 6 percent interest rate, draw an annual income of $9000, or $750 a month. In addition, we both had modest 401(k) rollover accounts that she could draw on if I died.

Thus, it seemed to us that Sara would be protected financially even if I took my maximum pension and left her no *Post* pension. So we did it. Sara signed off on the deal—something she was required to do by law. The federal government wants to be sure people are aware that if their spouses take a single life pension, they can be left without any pension income.

Having second thoughts

It is, of course, too late to change my decision, although I must tell you that—five years later—I am having some second thoughts about the idea of taking my maximum pension payment and not leaving any pension for Sara. My second thoughts arose recently, when I decided to figure out how our family income would change upon my death. So I added up how much money we now get from pensions and Social Security. The total from pensions (after tax is withheld and after other deductions) is $2893. The total from Social Security is $2600. The grand total is $5493 a month.

But see how the picture changes if I die:

First, Sara would lose her $1000 Social Security payment and get mine instead, because mine is higher. So she would get $1600 a month from Social Security. Add her GE pension of $707 (after tax is withheld and after other deductions), And the grand total is $2307.

That's a big difference. In fact, it is a $3186 difference between what we get together and what she'd get alone. If you count the $750 a month she would get from investing my insurance money, the difference drops to $2436, but that's still a 55 percent dip in income.

Hopefully, the money in our 401(k) rollover accounts would help provide Sara with some additional income. And her living expenses, as a single person, would be less than they are for the two of us together. But I think Sara's comfort level would be higher if she knew she would receive my pension for the rest of her life. Moreover, she wouldn't have to spend a lot of time managing investments or depending on others to do it for her. Nor would she have to worry about the health of the financial markets and whether her nest egg was being eroded.

So, after thinking about it, I have come to the conclusion that Sara would have been better off if I had taken the 100 percent spousal benefit. That would have given me a monthly check of $1900, and she would have continued to get the same check after I died. It would have been costly, of course: We would have given up $632 a month, and that would have made it harder for us to pay our bills. But it might have had advantages in future years.

Trying to outguess life

There is, of course, no way to know how long any of us are going to live; hence, speculating about what might happen in the future has its limitations. But let's try it, anyway. Let's try this scenario:

Let's say I retired at 69 and took a 100 percent spousal benefit of $1900 a month. And let's say I lived for 10 years after retirement. By taking the $1900 check instead of the full $2532, I would have lost $632 a month, or $7584 a year, or $75,840 for those 10 years.

If Sara then survived me for another 10 years, she would have gotten the same $1900 a month check. So she would have gotten the same $75,840 over the 10 years. Essentially, we would have broken even. What I gave up, she would get back. But more than that, she would have had the security of knowing she was getting a regular pension check. And I think that's important.

Perhaps if I had thought all this through more carefully at the time I retired, I might have made a different decision on how to take my pension. The point of this story, though, is that the decision regarding how to take your pension is not a simple one: It has many more dimensions than I realized at the time I retired—and many more dimensions than you might realize.

Every pension plan is somewhat different. Therefore, every plan will have different options. For instance, *The Washington Post* plan does not offer a lump-sum option. But many pension plans do. Thus, you may have to choose between taking your pension in one lump sum or in monthly payments.

That lump-sum option has some pros and cons, which are summarized in one of my favorite reference books, *The Vanguard Guide to Investing During Retirement* (New York: McGraw-Hill, 1998). Here they are:

Taking a lump-sum payment

Pros

Taking a lump sum enables you to make your own decisions on how you want to invest your money. As a result, you may be able to draw a higher income from your investments than you would get from a monthly pension check. The money also would be available for an emergency or a business opportunity. Monthly pension checks end when you die or when your spouse dies. But the lump-sum money, if wisely invested, would still be there for your heirs.

Cons

The temptation to spend all or some your lump-sum money may be overwhelming. That's what happens to many people who get large amounts of money in lump-sum payments. Forty percent of workers aged 55 to 64 spend all or some of their lump-sum money, according to the U.S. Department of Labor. The other 60 percent put all their pension money into savings—a move that will help them pay for their living expenses in retirement. Moreover, the job of managing a large sum of money may involve more investment risk than you are either used to or comfortable with. And though you could derive more income from investing your money yourself, you also could get less if the investment climate is unfavorable. In addition, your lump-sum payment is likely to be fully taxable, which would give you a large tax bite in one year and thus reduce the amount of money you will have available to invest. However, you can postpone the taxes due on your lump-sum payment by rolling over the entire amount to an IRA. The money then can continue to grow on a tax-deferred basis until you are ready to take it out.

Taking a monthly payment

Pros

The process is simple: Once you've decided on which option to choose—single life or a spousal benefit—the rest is automatic. You know how much you'll be getting each month, making it easy to draw up your retirement budget and to plan for taxes. Gyrations in the stock market or bond market won't be a worry, since your income is set. And if you're lucky enough to have a long retirement, those monthly payments will add up.

Cons

Pension plans generally are not adjusted for inflation. Thus, you could steadily lose purchasing power over the years. At an inflation rate of 3.5 percent, you would lose half your purchasing power in 20 years. And once you've taken your pension as a monthly payment—also called an annuity—you can't change it. Further, your pension ends when you die or when your spouse dies. That means there won't be any pension money to leave to your heirs.

In any event, Mike Bahr of the *Post* helped me put together a list of the things that a future retiree should think about before making pension decisions. Here they are:

- Talk to the benefits expert in your company and ask for an explanation of the formula that your pension plan uses to determine how much money you will get when you retire. It may be possible to schedule your retirement in a way that will help you get a larger benefit. If, for instance, you expect a sizable pay raise in the next two years, it might be worth staying on the job to boost your average pay history—which could raise the amount of your pension.

- When talking to the benefits expert, get a copy of the various monthly payment options that will be available to you. Take time to study them, and think about the implications of giving up income now to leave income for your spouse in the future.
- Remember that your pension is considered by the IRS to be income and thus is fully taxable. Most pension plans will withhold taxes if you if you request that option. But, of course, tax withholding and deductions for health or life insurance will reduce the amount of money you will get in each check. Thus, in planning your retirement budget, use your "net" pension amount, not your gross.
- If you decide to roll over your lump-sum payment into an IRA, make sure that the rollover is made directly to the mutual fund, brokerage firm, or other company that you will choose for your IRA account. The most efficient way is to have your employer send the money directly to the company handling your account. That avoids taxes and penalties.

If you tell your employer to give you the money first—called an "indirect rollover" the employer will withhold 20 percent for taxes, and you will have 60 days to open the IRA account. And when you do, you will have to make up the 20 percent from your own pocket. While you can get the 20 percent back eventually, you'll have to file a tax form to do so. So spare yourself that hassle by doing a direct rollover. Make the arrangements in advance with your company and the institution that you choose for your IRA.

- Before making any final decisions, consider the state of your health and that of your spouse. If you or your spouse have health problems that may shorten your normal longevity, consider those factors when making your pension choices.
- Consider, too, your overall financial situation, and try to choose a pension option that best fits that situation. If you

take the maximum pension, as I did, will your spouse have enough other income coming in—or savings to draw on—to make ends meet when your pension stops? If you have limited savings, and you need Social Security and pension income to support you, you may want to make sure that your spouse continues to get a pension check after your death, even if you have to take a lower monthly payment to do so.

· Think about your family obligations. Are there children or other relatives who depend on you for financial help? Those obligations may influence your decision regarding which pension payment option to take.

Finding a lost pension

Ordinarily, when you decide to retire and take your pension, all you need to do is to walk down the hall at work and talk to the benefits person. But suppose that after you've done that, you remember that 25 years ago you left a smaller company which also had a pension plan. Now that you're retiring, you wonder if you're entitled to a pension from your previous employer.

So you decide to call the company. You look in the phone book. The company is not listed. You call directory assistance. It doesn't have a listing either. You call the chamber of commerce. None of its people ever heard of the company. You try everything you can think of, but you can't find the company.

It doesn't seem like it would be that easy for a company to disappear. But it happens all the time, especially in the era of mergers and acquisitions. According to the Pension Benefit Guaranty Corp. (PBGC), a federal agency, "Thousands of retired workers in the United States are entitled to pension payments that they have not claimed because they do not know where to look."

As the PBGC points out in its useful booklet, *Finding a Lost Pension*, a company may

- Move from one town to another
- Close a plant and consolidate its operations elsewhere
- Be bought by another company and be given a new name
- Merge with another company
- Divide into separate units, none of which keeps the original company name
- Go bankrupt
- Close its doors and go out of business

But even if a company has disappeared, it doesn't mean the company's pension plan also has disappeared. In many cases, the PBGC says, the money is sitting safely in a fund somewhere, waiting for the worker, or perhaps a surviving spouse, to come forward and claim it.

Helping people find "missing pensions" is one of the many responsibilities of the PBGC. The federal agency was created by the Employee Retirement Income Security Act of 1974 (ERISA) to encourage the continuation of defined benefit pension plans, provide timely and uninterrupted payment of pension benefits, and keep pension insurance premiums at a minimum. Currently, PBGC insurance protects the retirement benefits of 43 million workers. Because of that insurance, these workers will get their pensions even if their employer goes out of business or the plan runs out of money.

The PBGC's "Pension Search" program may help you locate a "missing" pension. But there are a couple of things you need to think about before you start looking. A key question is, Were you vested in the company's pension plan before you left the company? Being vested means that no matter when you leave a job, you are eligible to receive a pension when you retire. If you weren't vested, you may not have a chance to claim benefits.

Today, most pension plans require five years of employment before vesting. Prior to the mid-1980s, plans typically required 10 years of service to vest. Prior to the mid-1970s, it was 20 years.

Also, before 1976, to get a pension, you could be required to work for the same employer until you actually retired.

Indeed, from 1952 to 1971, I worked for a company in which you joined the pension plan at age 30, but you did not vest and thus could not get your pension until you retired at age 65, some 35 years later. If you left the company anytime before age 65, you got your own contribution back, plus 3 percent interest. And so, when I left the company at the age of 44, I lost about 14 years of pension benefits. Under ERISA, that type of plan is no longer permitted.

ERISA also created other, broad protections that helped prevent workers from losing their pensions. The Department of Labor monitors pension plans to make sure that they are solvent and being managed properly. The Internal Revenue Service also regulates pension plans.

As mentioned earlier, the fact that a company has vanished doesn't mean that the pension plan has vanished, too. Many things could have happened to the plan. The PBGC notes that

- Despite reorganizations and mergers, the original plan may be intact. Those who run what today is left of the old company may still have a legal obligation to pay benefits due under the old plan.
- The plan may have bought an annuity from an insurance company, which undertook the obligation to pay annuities to everyone entitled to benefits under the plan.
- The plan may have been taken over by the PBGC, which will pay benefits up to certain limits.
- If a plan was terminated by the employer and benefits were paid to those employees who could be found, benefits for "missing" participants may have been turned over to PBGC for its Pension Search program.

So it may be possible for you to find your "missing pension" after all. However, it may take quite a bit of research. Suggestions on how to conduct a search for a "missing pension" are contained in the PBGC publication *Finding a Lost Pension.* For a free copy, write to Pension Benefit Guaranty Corp., Communications and Public Affairs Department, 1200 K St. NW, Washington, D.C. 20005-4026. The information also is available on the Internet at www.pbgc.gov

The PBGC's Web site also allows you to search electronically for a "missing" pension. You can search under your own name or under the company name. Click on the "Pension Search" button on the PBGC Web page, www.pbgc.gov

For more information

- The Pension Benefit Guaranty Corporation (PBGC). A government agency, the PBGC ensures that workers get their pension benefits and helps people find "lost pensions." www.pbgc.gov
- The U.S. Department of Labor. This agency's Web site offers information on pensions and other matters of interest to retirees. www.dol.gov
- The Employee Benefit Research Institute (EBRI). A research and education group, EBRI seeks to enhance the development of sound employee benefit programs. www.ebri.org
- American Savings Educational Council (ASEC). A coalition of public- and private-sector institutions, ASEC promotes savings and retirement planning. www.asec.org
- AARP. The nation's largest organization for retirees and pre-retirees, AARP has a Web site that contains a wide range of pension-related information. www.aarp.org

DECISION 5

What should I do with the money in my company savings plan?

During the years that I worked at *The Washington Post*, I partici-
pated in the paper's 401(k) savings plan. The plan, offered by
many U.S. companies, was created by Uncle Sam to encourage
American workers to save for retirement and other financial goals.
These kinds of plans vary from company to company, but here is
how the plan worked at the *Post*:

As an employee, I set aside a portion of my salary for savings—
we were paid every two weeks—and the paper automatically
deposited that money in my account. In my later years at the
paper, I put about 9 percent of my pay into the 401(k) account.

The savings plan had several great features. To begin with, the
amount of money I earmarked for savings was deducted from my
pay before my income taxes were calculated and withheld. That
reduced my taxable earnings each payday and thus also reduced
my income taxes for the year. So, in a sense, I was doing two things
at once: saving money regularly and also saving on income taxes.
I thought that was a pretty good deal.

But it got even better. After I made my regular contribution
to the savings plan, the *Post* put in its contribution, called "a company match." In my later years at the paper, the match represented
4.5 percent of my pay, or about half of my contribution.

Finally, the paper gave me several choices about how I wanted
to invest the money in my account. I studied the list of available
funds and decided to put my contributions into the Vanguard
Windsor mutual fund, one of several stock funds that were offered
to *Post* employees. I also decided to use the company's matching
money to buy *Washington Post* stock.

Over the years, I became convinced that the 401(k) plan
is a powerful way to save for retirement. It has several major
advantages:

- Your contribution goes directly into your savings plan
  before it is taxed. Thus, 100 cents of every dollar that you put
  into the plan goes to work. The contribution also reduces
  your income taxes for that year.

- The company's matching contribution is "free money" (although at some companies the match may be considered by management to be part of workers' overall benefits). In any event, the company contribution increases the amount of dollars that you have in your account. And those dollars also grow on a tax-deferred basis.

- Many companies let you invest your savings in mutual funds. That means that your money will be managed by investment professionals who are likely to make your money grow over a period of years. Essentially, your money makes money—a wonderful bit of arithmetic called "compounding" that was so admired by Prof. Albert Einstein, as noted in Chapter 2.

- No taxes are due on your savings or on any of the gains in your 401(k) plan until you begin to withdraw the money. However, as mentioned earlier, when you take out money that has not been taxed before, it will be taxed at ordinary income tax rates. In my case, I began to take money out of my account when I turned 70½, as required by the IRS. We'll talk about how to make your withdrawals in Chapter 6.

Looking back, I can see that being able to participate in the *Post*'s 401(k) plan for many years made a significant difference in the amount of money I had available for my retirement years. The same was true for Sara, who saved her money in a 401(k) plan at GE.

My gratitude for our 401(k) plans, however, does not change the warning I issued in Chapter 2 about the impact of taxes on retirees. While people should take maximum advantage of the 401(k) plan, they should also be aware that after they retire and begin to take money out of their tax-deferred savings accounts, they will pay income taxes on those withdrawals. And they should set aside money to pay those taxes.

As Sara and I discovered, the tax bite can be rather large. Early in my retirement, it even became difficult to balance our family budget. I simply hadn't realized how much I would owe in taxes after taking money out of our 401(k) rollover accounts.

As mentioned earlier, if your income from pensions and Social Security totals $40,000 a year and you withdraw $10,000 from your IRAs, your total income will rise to $50,000. That is likely to increase your taxes for that year.

Despite the tax aspect, Sara and I urge anyone who has the opportunity to contribute to a retirement savings plan at work to do so. Sign up as soon as you're eligible. Put in as much money as you can afford, up to the limit allowed by the plan. Keep at it for many years, and you will be on your way to a comfortable retirement.

Turning workers into investors

For Sara and me, the 401(k) plan made it easy for us to save regularly and automatically year after year. In the days before we had our 401(k) plans, we would take each paycheck and try to carve out a small piece for our savings account. Depending on how many bills we had on our desk, the money would sometimes get into our saving account and sometimes not.

With the advent of the 401(k) plan, our savings efforts were put on automatic pilot. The money came out of our paychecks regularly and silently. We also got the benefit of matching money from our employers and tax deferral from Uncle Sam.

That was the good news about contributing to our 401(k) plans. The bad news—if you want to call it that—was that once you put money into a plan, you also have to decide how you want to invest the money. That sounds like it ought to be easy, but it's not: Making your own investment decisions can be a considerable responsibility, especially as your nest egg grows larger and larger over the years.

For instance, let's assume you earned $50,000 a year and put 6 percent of your salary ($250 a month) into your 401(k) plan. Your employer matched half of your contribution and put in another $125 a month. That made the total contribution $375 a month.

Let's also assume that you invested your savings in a Standard & Poor's (S&P) 500 Stock Index mutual fund for 20 years—namely, the decades of the 1980s and 1990s. During that period, the S&P 500's average annual total return was 18.87 percent a year, with dividends and capital gains reinvested. Then, by the end of the 20 years, your 401(k) plan would have accumulated $984,742—with a deduction for the expenses of the index fund.

My point is that people who know little about investing can wake up one day and find themselves with extremely large amounts of money in their 401(k) plans, simply because they were fortunate to have steady, well-paying jobs for 15 or 20 years or more. And yet they may not have a clue as to how to best preserve their savings in the volatile markets of the twenty-first century. We'll talk more about that in Chapter 7.

In many ways, the growth of the 401(k) plan, also called a defined contribution savings plan, has helped revolutionize the American financial system. Clearly, it helped fuel the boom in the mutual fund business. As of March 2000, there were 7869 mutual funds, which held $7.3 trillion, according to the Investment Company Institute (ICI), a mutual fund trade association based in Washington, D.C.

The 401(k) plan has been one of the fastest growing parts of the financial industry, with 401(k) assets increasing at about 18 percent a year, the ICI says. The group also notes that about 45 percent of 401(k) assets are invested in mutual funds. As of 1999, according to Cerulli Associates, Inc., there were 305,000 401(k) plans, holding $1.7 trillion belonging to 39.3 million participants. Most of those people must decide for themselves—from the choices that are available—where they're going to invest their money.

What does all this mean? In a practical sense, it means that millions of American workers who might never have owned a stock or even a mutual fund are now "in the market" and have a stake in how individual companies and markets perform. Those of us in the financial media—print, radio, and television—have seen an incredible growth in the size of the audience for news and information about financial markets.

Of course, while investing in stocks and bonds offers you a chance to share in the long-term growth of the American economy, it also forces you to share in the short-term gyrations of the financial markets. On Wall Street, traders are fond of saying, "The market climbs a wall of worry." Individual investors, too, often have to climb that same wall. One of the great challenges of long-term investing is to remain unemotional and committed to stay the course even when the markets are plummeting.

I can testify that even people with a knowledge of investing can act emotionally and make serious mistakes with their 401(k) money. I know because I did exactly that. This is my story:

My $70,000 investment mistake

In the 1980s I was investing my 401(k) money in the Windsor Fund, a value-oriented stock mutual fund that was part of the Vanguard Group. The Windsor Fund was one of the investment choices offered to *Post* employees. The fund provided a respectable return. During the six years I was in the fund, it gained an average of 11.8 percent a year, and my savings grew nicely.

But in 1990 I got very nervous about the safety of my nest egg. On August 2 Iraq invaded Kuwait, and the international scene became very unsettled. I thought that a war might be in the offing. The markets also became very volatile. The Dow Jones industrial average dropped 18 percent between August 1 and October 11, 1990, on fears that the United States might get into a Middle East battle. At the same time, the price of the shares in the Windsor Fund fell from $12.39 to $9.72, a drop of 22 percent.

I was dismayed by the loss in the value of my Windsor shares and concerned about whether the downdraft would get worse. So

I sold my shares and moved my money to a Vanguard money market fund. As it turned out, that was a bad mistake. In January 1991, when U.S. bombers struck Baghdad and returned without meeting significant resistance, the U.S. stock market came roaring back. The Dow ended 1991 with a gain of 20 percent, and the Windsor Fund rose 28.6 percent. But, of course, I was no longer in the fund. By leaving the fund when I did, I got the fund's losses, and I wasn't there to get any of the fund's gains when the price of a share went back up.

But that, unfortunately, is not the end of the story. Because of inertia or just a failure to pay attention to my financial affairs, I left my money in the money market fund for the next 5½ years, until I retired. During those years, the money market fund earned a paltry average of 4.6 percent a year, while the Windsor Fund turned in an annualized gain of 18 percent a year.

I now figure that the decision to move my money out of the stock fund and into the money market fund and leave it there for 5½ years cost me about $70,000. True, it was money I never actually had in my pocket. But if I had left the money in the Windsor Fund, I would have retired with an extra $70,000.

Naturally, my wife and friends wanted to know how a financial writer who was knowledgeable about the markets could make that kind of mistake. I don't have a good answer. But I did learn a valuable lesson: Don't try to outguess the market. Decide on your long-term investment strategy, and as long as it's the right strategy for you, stick to it.

The educated investor

When several of my friends heard about my $70,000 investment mistake, they tried to console me by confessing that they had made similar errors. "I know how you feel," they said, "I did the same thing myself." Frankly, it wasn't much consolation, but it was a reminder that millions of American workers are being called upon to make important investment decisions, often without much investment knowledge or experience. As a result, there is a huge need in this country for investor education. Fortunately, there are signs that employers are beginning to recognize this need. In recent years, companies that offer 401(k) plans have been steadily increasing the number of investment choices they offer employees, according to a 1999 survey of 491 employers by Hewitt Associates LLC, an international consulting firm. That year, sponsors offered workers an average of 11 investment options, up from 8 in 1997.

Wider choices will help members of 401(k) plans to diversify their investments—a positive development. But it also will mean that employees, faced with more investment options, will have to make more sophisticated choices. A majority of the companies surveyed said they already provide their workers with investment information. However, about half of the companies said they are developing plans to offer workers advice from outside investment sources.

The Hewitt executive who heads the firm's defined contribution practice, Scott Peterson, looks at the problem this way: "As employers offer more options in 401(k) plans, it is crucial that they also increase their efforts to help employees make the most of this benefit. Understanding how decisions made today affect their finances tomorrow is imperative if employees hope to have a stable financial future."

That would seem to be doubly important in light of what employers said about the investment skills of their employees. Nearly two thirds of employers surveyed in the 1999 Hewitt 401(k) Trends and Experience Survey said their workers were making at least three mistakes: investing too conservatively, not diversifying their investments adequately, and investing without sufficient knowledge.

Choosing what to do with your money

When you walk into the office of the benefits specialist at your company and announce that you are ready to retire, the specialist will tell you that you have several options regarding what to do with the money you have saved in your 401(k) plan.

If you have worked for 20 years or more and have been saving aggressively and investing thoughtfully, the amount in your savings account may be the largest pot of money you've ever had. If that is the case—and I hope it is—you will want consider your options very carefully. Assuming that you are over 59½, consider the following options.

A rollover IRA

This is the option that Sara and I both chose when we retired. Before Sara left GE, she opened an IRA rollover account at a major mutual fund company. GE then sent her a check for her 401(k) money that was made out to her and to the mutual fund company (which indicated that the money had to go into her account at the fund company).

Sara quickly took the check to the local office of the fund company and deposited the money in her account. Initially, she parked the money in a money market account. Afterward, she studied the available mutual funds and invested portions of her money in some of those funds. Her objective was to keep the money invested and to keep it working and growing.

When I retired from the *Post* a few years later, I did much the same thing. I opened an IRA rollover account at a major brokerage firm, and the *Post* sent me a check for my 401(k) money made out to me and to the brokerage company. I then deposited the check in my new rollover account, also initially in a money market fund. I chose a brokerage account because I wanted to invest in specific stocks rather than funds. Over the past few years, I have had my share of winners and losers in the stock market, but, like Sara, I achieved my main purpose, which was to keep the money invested and growing.

What happens to our savings is of great concern to us because we know we will have to depend on our 401(k) money to help pay for some of our retirement expenses in the years ahead. Doing a rollover IRA, I believe was the best way to deal with our 401(k) money. But there are other options, as well.

Indirect rollover IRA

In this scenario, your employer sends you a check for your 401(k) money, but the employer is required to withhold 20 percent of your money for income taxes—money that gets sent to the IRS. For instance, if you have $200,000 in your account, your employer would withhold $40,000 for the IRS and send you a check for $160,000. You will then have 60 days to open an IRA rollover account and deposit your money.

To avoid income taxes, you will be required to deposit the full $200,000 in your IRA rollover account. That means you will have to come up with the $40,000 your employer withheld for taxes out of your own pocket. If you don't, that amount will be treated as a taxable distribution. Eventually, you may be able to get your $40,000 back when you file your federal income tax return for the year of the distribution.

In short, the indirect rollover produces the same result as the direct rollover, but it comes with a lot of hassle for very little gain. About the only benefit of this strategy is that you have use of 80 percent of the money from your employer's plan for a maximum of 60 days. It hardly seems worth the trouble.

Whether you roll over your assets directly or indirectly to an IRA, the money in your 401(k) plan represents the money you and your employer put there, plus any gains on your investments.

These sums will all be considered pretax money, meaning money that has yet to be taxed. However, if you contributed any additional money to your account—money on which you already paid taxes—it will be given to you in a lump sum at the time the pretax 401(k) money is rolled over to an IRA.

A cash distribution

This is probably the worst thing you can do with your 401(k) money, because you will simply give up most of it in taxes. Here is an example of what can happen to your $200,000 if you take it all in cash:

First, your company will withhold 20 percent, or $40,000, as taxes for the IRS.

Second, let's assume that you are in the 31 percent bracket. Your employer has already withheld 20 percent. So you would owe another 11 percent of $200,000, or $22,000, if you withdraw the lump sum all at once.

Third, in addition to paying federal taxes, you will have to remit state and/or local taxes on your withdrawal. Suppose that these taxes cost you another 7 percent, or $14,000.

That all adds up to $76,000, leaving you only $124,000 from your original $200,000. That doesn't sound like a good way to handle money that you carefully saved for so many years.

But perhaps the most devastating effect of taking a cash distribution is that all your money loses its tax-deferred status and becomes fully taxable, which can be costly over the long term. The dramatic difference between what $200,000 will produce and what $124,000 will produce over long periods of time is shown in Table 5.1.

Leaving money in your 401(k) plan

Some 401(k) plans will permit you to leave your money in the plan, and some will not. Federal regulations say a company can

TABLE 5.1   Why It's Not a Good Idea to Take Your 401(k)
Money in Cash

Time Period	Growth of $200,000 Rollover Investment	Growth of $124,000 Cash Investment
10 years	$431,785	$267,706
15 years	$634,433	$393,348
20 years	$932,191	$577,958

Note: Assumes 8 percent return in both accounts. In addition, rollover account will grow on a tax-deferred basis, while cash account will be subject to annual federal and state taxes.

make you leave a plan if you have less than $5000 in your account. Typically, I am told, that means you can stay in many plans if you have at least $5000 there.

A word of caution, though: If you are retired and have left money in your plan, you will have to start taking withdrawals at age 70½. However, the question is, Will the plan let you calculate how much you want to take out? Or will the plan insist on doing it for you? If the latter is the case, the calculations used may not be the most favorable to your situation or that of your beneficiaries.

Nevertheless, keeping your money in the company plan might be a wise tax move, especially if you contributed a large amount of after-tax money. (After you contribute the maximum amount of tax-deferred money, some plans permit you to contribute after-tax money as well.) As mentioned earlier, when you roll over your 401(k) money to an IRA, your company will send you back your after-tax money in a lump sum. At that point, if you want to invest the money, you will have to put it in a taxable account. However, if it stays in the 401(k) plan, it will continue to grow on a tax-deferred basis. The longer you can keep it there, the less you will pay in income taxes.

Dealing with company stock

If your 401(k) plan allowed you to invest in company stock, you have several options. You can sell the stock within your 401 (k) plan, if that is permitted, and roll the total amount of money from your plan into an IRA rollover account, either directly or indirectly. Or you can keep the shares of stock and roll them over into an IRA account, along with any other money in your plan.

However, you may have company stock in your plan that has substantially increased in value over the years. (Indeed, let's hope you do!) If so, you may want to consider moving the stock to a taxable brokerage account when you roll over the balance of your 401(k) into an IRA, suggests financial planner Christine S. Fahlund at T. Rowe Price Associates. The primary reason for doing this would be to take advantage of capital gains tax rates, which may be considerably less than your ordinary income tax rates during retirement. The details get a bit tricky, but stay with me.

At the time the shares are taken from your 401(k) plan, you will pay ordinary income taxes only on the original cost basis of the shares, not on their fair market value. At a later point, if you decide to sell some of the shares that are in the brokerage account, you would then pay capital gains taxes on the total gains realized on the stock from the time they were purchased in the plan—but only at a 10 percent or 20 percent rate.

If you never sell the shares, the tax advantages get even better, Christine Fahlund says. This is what would happen:

When your heirs sell the shares, they will pay capital gains taxes only on the increase in the value of the shares that occurred while they were in your 401(k) plan and any increase in their fair market value after your death. But your heirs would not pay income tax on any gains that occurred between the time you moved the shares to your brokerage account and the date of your death. That is because, when you die, the cost basis of the shares is "stepped up"—as tax people like to say. This means that, for your heirs, the cost basis of your shares will be the price of the shares on the day you died. Thus, if they sell the shares immediately, there will be no additional gains to be taxed.

All in all, the 401(k) plan is like a good friend: It'll be there when you need it. But as with any friend, take time to get to know it well, and treat it with respect.

Saving in America: good news and bad

The good news about saving in America is that if you give employees a chance to contribute to a 401(k) plan, they are likely to do so. In a study of retirement savings in America, Ohio State University professor Catherine P. Montalto found that 86.6 percent of U.S. workers who have a 401(k) or similar plan available at work are contributing to those plans. She also found that 62 percent of U.S. households are saving money in various kinds of retirement accounts.

When I think about it, I realize that my wife and I were able to retire in large part because we saved money in our 401(k) plans at work. That money, together with the income it produces, helps pay for our monthly living expenses. But the important point is that we were able to save that money for two reasons:

- First, we worked for companies that offered 401(k) plans to their employees. Moreover, those companies were willing to match a portion of their employees' contributions.
- Second, we earned enough money at our jobs so that we were able to put a percentage of our salaries into our savings plans each month.

We were lucky. Millions of people in this country work at companies that do not offer 401(k) plans to their employees. Or if they do, they do not match the employee's contribution.

Generally speaking, savings plans tend to be more widely available at larger companies than at smaller firms. The same is true of pension plans. In addition, smaller firms tend to pay lower wages than bigger companies. Thus, many small-company employees are disadvantaged in a couple of ways: First, they have no 401(k) plans and no pension plans, and they are paid relatively low wages, making it difficult for them to find the money to invest in IRAs and other tax-deferred plans. Then, when these workers reach retirement age, they tend to draw relatively low Social Security benefits because they were relatively low-wage earners for most of their lives.

The full dimensions of this problem were revealed by Professor Montalto's recent study of the retirement savings of American households. She concluded that 56 percent of U.S. households with at least one employed householder will not be able to accumulate enough savings to maintain their preretirement living standard. Worse yet, her study showed that 11 percent of U.S. households will reach retirement with incomes that are below the national poverty threshold. The federal government considers an income of $10,070 a year to be the poverty level for a two-person household whose members are 65 or older. For a one-person household at 65 or more, the poverty level is $7990.

Clearly, millions of Americans appear to be headed for a dismal retirement unless they are able to save more than they do now. Encouraging low-income Americans to save more is a worthy, but understandably difficult, task. In the long run, higher savings will depend on higher wages and, in turn, on better education and improved job skills.

For more information

Bogosian, Wayne G. and Lee, Dee. *The Complete Idiot's Guide to 401(k) Plans.* MacMillan Distribution, 1998.

Iwaszko, Knute and O'Connell, Brian. *The 401(k) Millionaire.* Villard Books, New York, 1999.

Rowland, Mary. A Commonsense Guide to Your 401(k). Bloomberg Press, Princeton, NJ, 1997.

Slesnick, T. and Suttle, John C. *IRAs, 401(k)s, and Other Retirement Plans: Taking Your Money Out.* Nolo Press, Berkeley, CA, 1998.

DECISION 6

When do I have to take money out of my IRAs?

When I reached my seventieth birthday, my family and friends had a party to help me celebrate. But six months later, when I turned 70½, the only people celebrating were those at the IRS.

As mentioned earlier, 70½ is the age at which you are required by Uncle Sam to start withdrawing money from your IRAs and most other tax-deferred retirement accounts. (Roth IRAs are not included.) And, of course, you have to pay income taxes on that money. It's no wonder the tax collectors were so happy when I turned 70½. They had waited 20 years for those taxes.

For most of us, paying taxes on IRA withdrawals is a good-news, bad-news story. The good news is that we were wise to save money in tax-deferred retirement accounts for a long time. The bad news is that when it's time to take the money out, most or all of it will be taxable. In my case, it means that for every dollar I take out of my IRAs and spend, I have to take an extra 40 cents out of my non-IRA savings to pay my federal and state taxes.

That hurts, especially if you didn't anticipate that expense when you worked out your retirement budget. Unfortunately, I didn't. But hopefully, if you save regularly while you're working, and invest wisely, you should be able to pay your taxes and have money left over to help pay your living expenses.

However, whether you save a lot of money or a little money in a retirement account, the process of taking the money out—as Uncle Sam requires—is not a simple one, although it is easier than it used to be. That's because the IRS, in 2001 and again in 2002, simplified the way you calculate the amount of money you must take out of your IRAs each year. Even so, there are many parts of the process that will still strain your brain.

Of course, it helps to know the lingo. In the language used in the IRS regulations, withdrawals from IRAs are called "distributions." And the whole process of withdrawing money from retirement accounts at 70½ is known as taking your "Required Minimum Distributions" (RMDs).

Thus, if you run into a friend on the street who asks: "Have you taken you RMDs yet?" be assured that your friend is not asking about whether you've taken your vitamins recently—only whether you've made your IRA withdrawals yet.

Curiously, some mutual funds and financial companies use the phrase, "Minimum Required Distributions" (MRDs), while others use "Required Minimum Distributions" (RMDs). Why? Nobody seems to know. But I'm going to go with the IRS version-RMDs. After all, I say, "A tax by any other name is still a tax."

Simplifying the Rules

When the IRS announced its proposed new RMD rules –rules that are to become mandatory in 2003—it was a huge relief to retirees and financial advisers alike. The old rules, issued in 1987, were extremely complicated. It was difficult to figure out how much money you were supposed to take out of your IRA. And it was even more difficult to understand the rules concerning beneficiaries. The groans of frustrated taxpayers could be heard far and wide.

Someone at the IRS must have been listening. The new rules go a long way toward simplifying the process of figuring out one's withdrawals. Indeed, most taxpayers will have to consult only one simple IRS table—the Uniform Distribution Table (Table 6.1)— to find the number they need to calculate their withdrawals. Most IRA owners will use that table.

There is, however, one exception: In a case where your spouse is the sole beneficiary of your IRA for the entire year and your

TABLE 6.1 Uniform Distribution Table*

Your Age	Your Factor	Your Age	Your Factor
70	27.4	86	14.1
71	26.5	87	13.4
72	25.6	88	12.7
73	24.7	89	12.0
74	23.8	90	11.4
75	22.9	91	10.8
76	22.0	92	10.2
77	21.2	93	9.6
78	20.3	94	9.1
79	19.5	95	8.6
80	18.7	96	8.1
81	17.9	97	7.6
82	17.1	98	7.1
83	16.3	99	6.7
84	15.5	100	6.3
85	14.8		

*For use by owners of IRAs.
Source: Internal Revenue Service.

spouse is also more than 10 years younger than you are, you will use a different IRS table to locate your withdrawal. It's called the Joint Life and Last Survivor Expectancy table (Table 6.2).

The new IRS rules will have a two fold impact:

- First, they will reduce the amount of money that retirees are required to take out of their IRA accounts each year. That means that retirees will be able to keep more money in their accounts to help support them in retirement. It also means that when IRA owners die, they can leave greater sums to their heirs.

- Second, they also will allow people who inherit IRAs to stretch out withdrawals from the accounts over their own life expectancies. That could extend the "life" of IRAs for many years, especially if children or grandchildren are named as beneficiaries. The new rules also provide greater flexibility to IRA beneficiaries in the year following the owner's death.

Although the IRS has simplified the RMD withdrawal process, there are still some aspects that are complicated. For instance, the opportunity for your grandchildren or even great grandchildren to stretch out IRA accounts raises a number of important estate planning issues.

As a result, I strongly recommend that you consult a financial planner, an estate planner, or an accountant before you begin your withdrawals. Since RMD decisions affect not only your financial well being but also that of your heirs, it's important that they become part of an overall financial and estate plan. This is particularly true if you have large sums of money in your retirement plans.

MAKING YOUR FIRST WITHDRAWAL

When it comes to taking your first withdrawal, you have two options. The first option is to take your withdrawal in the year in which you are 70½. Or, if you wish, you can wait until April 1 of the following year for the initial withdrawal, and then take a second withdrawal by December 31 of that year. However, taking two withdrawals in the same year means that you will pay income tax on two withdrawals instead of one. I elected to take my first withdrawal when I was 70½ because I did not want to pay income tax on two withdrawals in one year.

If you take your withdrawal in the year in which you turn 70½, you will base it on how much money you had in your retirement account as of the previous December 31. As an example, let's say you reach 70½ in 2002. If you take your withdrawal in 2002, it would be based on the amount of money in your account on December 31, 2001.

Table 6.2 — Joint Life and Last Survivor Expectancy Table *

Spousal Beneficiary Age | Your Present Age
	70	71	72	73	74	75	76	77	78	79	80	81	82	83	84	85
50	35.1	35	34.9	34.8	34.8	34.7	34.6	34.6	34.5	34.5	34.5	34.4	34.4	34.4	34.3	34.3
51	34.3	34.2	34.1	34	33.9	33.8	33.8	33.7	33.6	33.6	33.6	33.5	33.5	33.5	33.4	33.4
52	33.4	33.3	33.2	33.1	33	33	32.9	32.8	32.8	32.7	32.7	32.6	32.6	32.6	32.5	32.5
53	32.6	32.5	32.4	32.3	32.2	32.1	32	32	31.9	31.8	31.8	31.8	31.7	31.7	31.7	31.6
54	31.8	31.7	31.6	31.5	31.4	31.3	31.2	31.1	31	31	30.9	30.9	30.8	30.8	30.8	30.7
55	30.3	30.9	30.8	30.6	30.5	30.4	30.3	30.3	30.2	30.1	30.1	30	30	29.9	29.9	29.9
56	29.5	30.1	30	29.8	29.7	29.6	29.5	29.4	29.3	29.3	29.2	29.2	29.1	29.1	29	29
57	28.8	29.4	29.2	29.1	28.9	28.8	28.7	28.6	28.5	28.4	28.4	28.3	28.3	28.2	28.2	28.1
58	28.1	28.6	28.4	28.3	28.1	28	27.9	27.8	27.7	27.6	27.5	27.5	27.4	27.4	27.3	27.3
59		27.9	27.7	27.5	27.4	27.2	27.1	27	26.9	26.8	26.7	26.6	26.6	26.5	26.5	26.4
60		27.2	27	26.8	26.6	26.5	26.3	26.2	26.1	26	25.9	25.8	25.8	25.7	25.6	25.6
61			26.3	26.1	25.9	25.7	25.6	25.4	25.3	25.2	25.1	25	24.9	24.9	24.8	24.8
62				25.4	25.2	25	24.8	24.7	24.6	24.4	24.3	24.2	24.1	24.1	24	23.9
63					24.5	24.3	24.1	23.9	23.8	23.7	23.6	23.4	23.4	23.3	23.2	23.1

Age											
64	23.6	23.4	23.2	23.1	22.9	22.8	22.7	22.6	22.5	22.4	22.3
65		22.7	22.5	22.4	22.2	22.1	21.9	21.8	21.7	21.6	21.6
66			21.8	21.7	21.5	21.3	21.2	21.1	21	20.9	20.8
67				21	20.8	20.6	20.5	20.4	20.2	20.1	20.1
68					20.1	20	19.8	19.7	19.5	19.4	19.3
69						19.3	19.1	19	18.8	18.7	18.6
70							18.5	18.3	18.2	18	17.9
71								17.7	17.5	17.4	17.3
72									16.9	16.7	16.6
73										16.1	16
74											15.4

* Use this table to determine your life expectancy factor only if your sole primary beneficiary is a spouse who is more than ten years younger than you are. To determine your 2003 RMD, divide your year-end retirement account balance as of December 31, 2002, by the divisor in the table above that corresponds to your age and your spouse's age as of December 31, 2003. For example, if you will be age 73 as of December 31, 2003 and your spouse will be age 62 as of that date, the life expectancy factor used to calculate your 2003 RMD would be 25.4.

Source: The Vanguard Group.

If you want to wait, you must take your first withdrawal by April 1, 2003. If you do that, the withdrawal will still be based on your account total as of December 31, 2001. However, if you do wait, you will then have to take a second withdrawal before December 31, 2003. In this case, the second withdrawal would be based on the amount of money in your account as of December 31, 2002.

Making a list

When you get close to 70½, it's a good time to ask yourself: "How many IRAs or other tax-deferred accounts do I have?" That's an important question because, when you make your withdrawals, you have to consider the assets in all those accounts. (Roth IRAs are not included.)

Here are some of the tax-deferred accounts that must be considered:

Traditional IRAs

A traditional IRA is a tax-deferred savings account for people who earn income. If you earn income, you also may contribute to a traditional IRA for a nonworking spouse. Contributions to traditional IRAs can be either deductible or nondeductible. A deductible contribution is so named because you were able to take an income tax deduction for the money you put into that account. The amount you put in, together with your gains, is taxable when you begin to take money out of that account. A nondeductible contribution is a contribution that you made with after-tax money. You did not receive a tax deduction when you made the contribution. Thus, only the gains on the earnings are taxable.

IRA rollover accounts

These are accounts that you set up when you roll over money from your 401(k) or similar retirement plan to an IRA account at a bank, brokerage, or mutual fund company.

Simplified Employee Pension Plan (SEP-IRA)

A retirement plan for sole proprietors, partners, or corporations. A SEP is set up as an individual employee retirement account, and the employer makes contributions to each separate account.

Savings Incentive Match Plan for Employees (SIMPLE-IRA)

A SIMPLE-IRA is a retirement plan for the self-employed or for a partnership or corporation with up to 100 employees. Employees can make pretax contributions from their pay; employers may make matching or nonmatching contributions.

Defined contribution plans (including profit-sharing and money purchase plans)

An employer contributes, perhaps, up to 25 percent of the total compensation of all eligible employees. In 2002, the most that can go to a single employee is 100 percent of the person's pay, or $40,000, whichever is less. The same holds true for a money purchase plan. After 2002, the $40,000 limit will be indexed to inflation, and will increase in $1000 increments. If you are at least 50 years of age, you can also make a "catch-up" contribution to the plan.

Company 401(K) plan

If an employee who retires leaves money in a company 401(k) plan, when the individual reaches 70½, he or she must begin to withdraw money from the retirement account. However, the rules of a particular 401(k) plan may affect how the withdrawals can be made.

403(b) plan

The 403(b) plan is generally available to employees of tax exempt organizations such as colleges, universities, hospitals, and charitable groups. Certain mandatory withdrawal rules apply to these plans as well.

Don't give up yet

Once you have figured out how many tax deferred accounts you own, make a list of those accounts and your balances as of the previous December 31. The next step is to find out how money you must take out of each account in the first year of your RMDs.

To do that, you will have to use one of two IRS life expectancy tables that will tell you the minimum amount you must withdraw in the first year. The IRS goal is to make sure you take out some of your retirement money each year and pay the income taxes due on that money. If you die before the end of your withdrawal period, your beneficiary will have the option to continue withdrawing annual payments from the account beginning in the year following your death. Note that your beneficiary, like you, can always take more, but never less, than the minimum required amount each year. Otherwise, penalties will apply.

When a husband dies, his widow-beneficiary can roll over the IRA into her own IRA and use the favorable Uniform Distribution

Table (Table 6.1). This table will show you the divisor to use when you figure out your withdrawals.

Locate your age. The number next to your age will be the divisor.

If you are using the Joint Life and Last Survivor Expectancy Table (Table 6.2), use your age and the age of your beneficiary to locate your divisor.

To calculate your withdrawals, divide the amount of money in each of your retirement accounts by your divisor. That's where your list will come in handy. The IRS says that you must do the calculation for each of your accounts.

Here's how it works: If you own four deductible IRAs, each with balances of $20,000 as of December 31, 2001, and your withdrawal factor is 26.2, you will have to withdraw a minimum of $763 from each of the four accounts, or a total of $3052. You may take the money out of one account or more than one account. But wherever it comes from, it is 100 percent taxable.

So, let's assume you have a fifth IRA—a nondeductible one. You contributed $10,000 in after-tax dollars to this account. And over the years, it gained another $10,000, for a total of $20,000. Under IRS rules, the $10,000 you contributed is not taxable.

So what do you do? Under this scenario, according to financial planner Christine S. Fahlund at T. Rowe Price Associates, you must total up the value of all your accounts. In this case the total is $100,000 (five accounts of $20,000 each). Then you have to figure out what portion of your withdrawals is not taxable.

Here's how the arithmetic goes: Of the $100,000 in your accounts, $10,000, or 10 percent, was contributed in after-tax money. We already know that you have to withdraw $763 from each account—or a total of $3815 (five accounts multiplied by $763). However, only 90 percent is taxable.

For each of the $763 withdrawals, you would have to pay taxes on only $687. Thus, for the five accounts, the total taxable amount of the withdrawals would be $3435 (five accounts multiplied by $687). The other $380 comes out income tax free.

When I made my first IRA withdrawal, I tried to be careful to take the right amount. While you are allowed to take out more than the minimum, you'd better not take less, or you could wind up paying a hefty penalty to the IRS. The penalty is 50 percent of the difference between the amount of money you withdrew and the amount that you should have taken out. And then, after paying the penalty, you must still withdraw the correct amount and pay the tax due on that amount.

How to use the life-expectancy tables

As I noted, the IRS gives you two tables to help you figure out your withdrawals. But the IRS also provides a third table that is intended for use by your beneficiaries after your death.

Here is a run down on how these tables are to be used. (For the purpose of this discussion, we will use a $100,000 IRA as an example).

Table 6.1 is the Uniform Distribution Table. It is the table that will be used by most individuals who must withdraw money from their IRA and tax-deferred accounts.

At age 70½, your divisor would be 27.4 Divide $100,000 by 27.4, and you get $3649 the amount of your initial minimum withdrawal.

Table 6.2 is the Joint Life and Last Survivor Expectancy Table. This should be used in cases where your spouse is the sole beneficiary of your account and is more than 10 years younger than you are.

For instance, if you are 73 and your spouse is 62—or 11 years younger—the table shows that your divisor is 25.4 If your account is worth $100,000, your first-year withdrawal would be $100,000 divided by 25.4, or $3937.

Table 6.3, the Single Life Expectancy Table, is to be used by nonspouse beneficiaries. Let's say that John, 74, dies when his daughter, Mary, is 41. Mary is John's beneficiary on his IRA account. In the year following John's death, Mary, now 42, consults the table and finds that her divisor is 41.7, meaning that she can take withdrawals from John's IRA account for more than 40 years. If the account balance was $100,000 on December 31 of the year of John's death, Mary's first withdrawal would be $2398 ($100,000 divided by 41.7).

Summing Up

Well, those are the bare bones of the process for taking IRA withdrawals. If you are embarking on this process, my advice is to start early, study your options carefully, and get all the advice you can find. You'll get through it. Then, along with me, you will wonder: Why is retirement such hard work?

For more information

- The IRS life expectancy tables are contained in IRS publication No. 590, "Individual Retirement Arrangements." To order the booklet, call 1-800-829-3676. You can also download the publication from the IRS Web site: www.irs.gov.
- The Vanguard Group publishes a useful booklet: "Taking Required Minimum Distributions." It is available from the Vanguard Retirement Resoures Center by calling 1-800-608-

Table 6.3 — Single Life-Expectancy Table *

Age	Life Expectancy	Age	Life Expectancy
0	82.4	53	31.4
1	81.6	54	30.5
2	80.6	55	29.6
3	79.7	56	28.7
4	78.7	57	27.9
5	77.7	58	27.0
6	76.7	59	26.1
7	75.8	60	25.2
8	74.8	61	24.4
9	73.8	62	23.5
10	72.8	63	22.7
11	71.8	64	21.8
12	70.8	65	21.0
13	69.9	66	20.2
14	68.9	67	19.4
15	67.9	68	18.6
16	66.9	69	17.8
17	66.0	70	17.0
18	65.0	71	16.3
19	64.0	72	15.5
20	63.0	73	14.8
21	62.1	74	14.1
22	61.1	75	13.4
23	60.1	76	12.7
24	59.1	77	12.1
25	58.2	78	11.4
26	57.2	79	10.8
27	56.2	80	10.2
28	55.3	81	9.7
29	54.3	82	9.1
30	53.3	83	8.6
31	52.4	84	8.1
32	51.4	85	7.6
33	50.4	86	7.1
34	49.4	87	6.7
35	48.5	88	6.3
36	47.5	89	5.9
37	46.5	90	5.5
38	45.6	91	5.2
39	44.6	92	4.9
40	43.6	93	4.6
41	42.7	94	4.3
42	41.7	95	4.1
43	40.7	96	3.8
44	39.8	97	3.6
45	38.8	98	3.4
46	37.9	99	3.1
47	37.0	100	2.9
48	36.0	101	2.7
49	35.1	102	2.5
50	34.2	103	2.3
51	33.3	104	2.1
52	32.3	105	1.9
		106	1.7
		107	1.5
		108	1.4
		109	1.2
		110	1.1
		111+	1.0

* For use by beneficiaries
Source: Internal Revenue Service

8615. You can also download the publication at the Vanguard Web site: www.vanguard.com

· T. Rowe Price Associates publishes "The IRA Minimum Required Distribution Guide." For a copy call, 1-888-421-0563. You also can request the publication on the company's Web site: www.troweprice.com

How should I invest during retirement?

Three years after I retired, I was shocked to discover that if my wife and I didn't cut down on our spending and get better results on our investments, we would use up all our retirement savings within eight years. As you can imagine, that was extremely bad news, because at that point, I was only 72 and my wife Sara was 70. In eight years, I would be only 80 and Sara would be 78—not terribly old by today's standards. In fact, Sara and I have many friends who are 80 and older and still lead active, interesting lives.

The truth of the matter is that I was hoping our savings would last until we were in our nineties. But my calculations told me we would fall far short of that goal.

Now, I'm not suggesting that if we used up our savings, we would be penniless. Sara and I are fortunate to have regular retirement incomes. Together with our Social Security benefits, our pension checks help pay for our basic living expenses. However, we use our savings to take occasional vacation trips and to otherwise enjoy our retirement. Without any savings to draw upon, our activities would be very limited.

How did I discover that our savings were dwindling rapidly? By using one of those "retirement calculators" that are so popular on the Internet. I went on line to the Web site operated by Vanguard mutual funds, www.vanguard.com. I located the company's retirement planning page and found a program that calculates how long your retirement savings will last. (The Vanguard computer program is one of several such programs available from financial service companies. A list is included at the end of the chapter.)

I then entered my financial information, responding to questions that appeared on my screen. When I was finished, I clicked on the "calculate" button, and the machine went to work. It digested my numbers and quickly rendered its verdict. It told me that I would use up all my savings by 2007. That was only eight years away.

The cause of the problem soon became apparent: We were dipping into our savings too often and not earning enough on our investments to replace the money being taken out. And, of course, as our nest egg shrank, the less it earned. Although I didn't like what the computer told me, I was grateful to get the warning in time to do something about it.

The first thing I did was to look at some "what if" calculations. I tried several different scenarios to see what I could do to make our savings last longer. I lowered our monthly expenses and raised the earnings on our investments. That seemed to help. The revised numbers had the effect of stretching out our savings for a few additional years.

But then I realized I had told the computer I would continue to work as a freelance writer until I was 90. On reflection, that seemed to be a bit of a stretch, so I went back and told the computer I would stop earning additional income at age 80. That made the picture worse.

The calculations left me with little choice but to think seriously about how much money Sara and I could save if we trimmed our living expenses. If that's what we have to do in the next few years, we'll do it. But, frankly, it's not a happy prospect.

Making ends meet

To put some of my findings in perspective, I talked with Richard W. Stevens, a principal at Vanguard, who supervises the firm's financial planning operations. Helping people learn how to invest during retirement is one of Stevens's main jobs.

While many retirees spend time worrying about investment risk, Stevens said, he believes that retirees should focus instead on cash flow. The main question facing retirees, he said, is "Where is the money coming from to help you pay your monthly expenses?"

If there is not enough money coming in, Stevens tells his clients, they've got to do one of two things: cut their expenses or increase their investment income—the latter even if it entails more risk. For many retirees, Stevens said, the question is not "How much risk can I afford to take?" The real question is "How much risk do I have to take to make ends meet?"

Stevens said older investors often worry too much about the impact of market downturns on their investments. Unless investors need their money soon and are forced to sell stocks in a falling market, he said, they generally can wait for the markets to recover from a correction.

Stevens noted that while there have been many one-year losses in the stock and bond markets—and even some negative two-year periods—there have been very few negative three- or four-year periods. Thus, he believes, the real danger that most retirees face is not a market crash, but running out of money.

Making your savings last

I wish now that I had run my finances through the Vanguard calculator long before I retired. I would have had a much more realistic idea of how much money we would need to pay our expenses through a 15- to 20-year retirement. I also would have tried harder to improve the returns on our investments.

Until you retire, I discovered, you don't think much about the difference between managing your money in retirement and managing it while you're working. When you're working—and saving for retirement—you pay your bills from your salary or wages. And you try your best to let your savings sit there and grow. But when you retire and you lose your regular paycheck, you are dependent on Social Security and pension checks—if you have a pension—and income from savings. You may also need to work part time to help out.

If you have maximized your income and minimized your expenses and you still face a gap between what's coming in and what's going out, you will have to see whether it is possible to earn more from your investments. You will have to think carefully about the money in your retirement savings accounts, how that money is invested, what it earns, and how much you can reasonably withdraw each year without seriously reducing the earnings potential of your nest egg. Figure 7.1 shows you how long your money will last, depending on the percent you earn each year and the percent you withdraw each year. Plot the number of years remaining by picking your savings growth rate and your rate of withdrawal. (The chart assumes that you are not adding to your savings.) The number at the intersection of these two rates is how many years may be left until your savings are depleted. For example, if your savings grow 3 percent annually and you withdraw your original principal at a rate of 10 percent annually, your savings may last roughly 12 years.

There are three main ways to invest your retirement savings: You can invest for growth, for income, or for a combination of growth and income. At the end of this chapter, you will find some suggestions on how to use your savings to provide a flow of monthly income and some growth as well.

Investing is a highly personal matter involving your financial needs, your time horizon, and your willingness to take risk. That being the case, I believe it's wise for each investor to discuss his or her goals with a financial planner or investment adviser. If you are already retired, an adviser can help you figure out how long your money will last in retirement. If you are still working, an adviser can help you develop an investment plan that will help you reach your goals. Suggestions on how to find a financial planner appear at the end of the chapter.

In the meantime, I am happy to share with you some of the lessons I have learned from my years of investing, watching the market, and making investment mistakes. If you expect to depend on your savings to help support you in retirement, these are lessons you, too, will need to learn. So here they are:

Figure 7.1 table — Savings growth rate (rows) vs. Withdrawal rate (columns):

Savings growth rate	\ Withdrawal rate 2%	3%	4%	5%	6%	7%	8%	9%	10%	11%	12%	13%	14%	15%	16%
15%															20
14%														21	16
13%													22	16	14
12%												23	17	14	12
11%											24	18	15	13	11
10%										25	19	15	13	12	10
9%									27	20	16	14	12	11	10
8%								29	21	17	14	12	11	10	9
7%							31	22	18	15	13	11	10	9	9
6%						33	24	19	16	14	12	11	10	9	8
5%					37	26	20	17	14	12	11	10	9	8	8
4%				41	28	22	18	15	13	12	10	9	9	8	7
3%			47	31	23	19	16	14	12	11	10	9	8	8	7
2%		55	35	26	20	17	15	13	11	10	9	8	8	7	7
1%	70	41	29	22	18	15	13	12	11	10	9	8	7	7	6

Withdrawal rate

Figure 7.1 When Will Your Savings Run Out? (Source: Oppenheimer Funds, Inc. This chart is intended as educational material about savings and investing and does not predict or depict the rate of return on any mutual fund or other investment. Consult an investment professional for a more specific and detailed analysis of your personal financial situation.)

Five golden rules
You must learn how to invest

If you are still working and belong to a 401(k) or other company savings plan, you are probably making decisions regarding how to invest your money by choosing from among a small number of investments offered by your company. If you are retired, you still have to make investment choices, but now you can choose from 7869 mutual funds, at least 5000 stocks, and countless bonds. And that can be mind boggling.

In either case, if you haven't already done so, it is time to learn how to invest. It is pretty obvious that knowing how to invest is now a required life skill in American society. The ability to save and invest wisely will enable millions of the elderly to have a decent lifestyle while they are living into their eighties and beyond. I can foresee the day when the four educational basics will be reading, writing, arithmetic—and investing.

Learning to invest is not difficult. Start with some of the popular investment magazines and TV stations that devote every day to covering the financial markets. Take a look at some of the many investment Web sites. Dozens of books and videos offer insights into investing. Remember this: Before you invest your money, invest your time and learn the basics of investing. It's not hard and it can even be fun. But start now. You owe it to yourself.

The greater the risk, the greater the reward

As surely as day follows night, the one rule that never changes on Wall Street is that risk and reward go hand in hand. The greater the risk, the greater the reward; and the greater the reward, the greater the risk. It sounds like a warning you might have gotten from a social studies teacher in high school, but anybody who has been burned in the financial markets knows the old rule is true. You simply can't get huge gains without taking huge risks. And what goes up very fast can also come down very fast, as the collapse of high-flying

Internet stocks proved during the spring of 2000. When you make any investment, always try to understand the risks you are taking.

Never try to outguess the market

Those of us who have been investing for a number of years know the truth of this statement. Remember, in Chapter 5, my tale of losing $70,000 in my 401(k) plan? As I discovered, if you sell everything and get out of the market because you think it is going down, chances are that you will sell at the lowest point and be out of the market when it rebounds. Thus, you will get the losses and miss the gains. Experienced investors know that the long-term trend of the market is up and that if you ignore the short-term gyrations and stay invested, you will benefit from those long-term upward movements.

Go for the averages

One of the most tantalizing rules of investing is "Buy low and sell high." It sounds easy, but it's a very hard thing to do on a consistent basis, as experienced traders will tell you. For investors like you and me, the next best thing is something called "dollar cost averaging." This involves investing the same amount of money in, say, a mutual fund every month over a long period of time. As the price of the fund's shares rise and fall, you will sometimes buy at the highs and sometimes at the lows. But in the long run, you will be buying your shares at an average price, which is a good deal. In any event, it certainly beats trying to decide when the right time is to buy those shares, since you are likely to guess wrong.

Spread your risk

As kids, we learned the old rule "Don't put all your eggs in one basket." Why? Because if you drop your basket, good-bye eggs. Thus, it makes sense to put your eggs in more than one basket.

That rule has turned out to be good advice for investors, too. People on Wall Street have their own word for it. They call it "diversification." Decades of experience have shown that your best chance to succeed as an investor is to put portions of your money into several different kinds of investments.

Specifically, diversification generally means putting some of your money in stocks, some in bonds, and some in money market funds. Within each category, you also will have a number of choices. For instance, you can invest in stocks of big companies or stocks of small companies, stocks of domestic firms or stocks of foreign firms. As regards bonds, you can choose among government bonds, corporate bonds, municipal bonds, and others. Money market funds vary in their interest rates, but they are basically similar to one another.

The theory of diversification rests on the fact that different types of investments march to the beat of different drummers. When stocks are going up, bonds may be going down, or vice versa. Similarly, when domestic stocks are rising, foreign stocks may be falling. In short, different investments behave differently at different times and, of course, give you different results. By spreading your money around, you can reduce your chances of being hurt financially if one sector of the market should take a big hit.

One note of caution, however: Some investors try to diversify by buying shares in many mutual funds. That may work if the funds have been carefully selected to represent different areas of the investment world, such as large companies, small companies, domestic companies, international companies, and so on. But all too often investors unknowingly buy several funds that all specialize in, say, large-cap value stocks. While the fund names are different, the investment philosophies are the same. Thus, instead of getting diversification, the investor gets a similar result from each of the funds—and more risk than anticipated.

Beyond the golden rules

Once you are comfortable with the idea of diversification, you will want to think about what portions of your money you want to put into stocks, bonds, and money market funds. Here again, Wall Street has an apt phrase. It's called "asset allocation."

Slicing the investment pie

There are many ways to slice your investment pie. You can cut it in three pieces—one for stocks, one for bonds, and one for money market funds. You can cut it in half and put 50 percent in stocks and 50 percent in bonds. Or you can put 50 percent in stocks, 40 percent in bonds, and 10 percent in money funds. You get the idea.

But why does it matter how you allocate your money? Earlier, we talked about diversification and how spreading your money around in different investments was your best protection against the short-term ups and downs of the market. Now, let's look at "asset allocation." By my definition, that's a strategy which advises us to lean in the same direction as the market. If stocks appear to be in an uptrend, let's switch some of our bond money to stocks. Instead of being 50-50 in stocks and bonds, we'll be 80 percent in stocks and 20 percent in bonds.

Professional investors spend a lot of time trying to decide how to allocate their money. If they correctly judge the direction of stocks or bonds, they will do well. And so can you. Becoming an informed investor will help you develop a sense of how the financial markets are moving. And that can help you make intelligent and profitable investment decisions.

Retirees—a special case

For many years, the common wisdom in the investment world was that stocks were suitable for younger investors, but not for older investors. The theory was that once you reached retirement age, you had to become more conservative and move your money into bonds and other fixed-income investments, which were judged to be less risky. The thinking was that retirees had to be wary of investing in stocks because, in the event of a market crash, they would lose the savings they needed to live on and might not have time to wait for the market to return to higher ground.

During the decades of the 1980s and 1990s, that view of retirement investing was replaced by another view, which holds that retirees no longer should give up their stocks and move all their money into bonds when they turn 65. In fact, it's now believed that it makes perfect sense for retirees to keep a significant percentage of their money in equities. And here is why:

THE LONGEVITY CASE

The Census Bureau tells us that the average 65-year-old can look forward to 15 years or more in retirement. Many retirees live into their eighties and even nineties. This is a huge change in life expectancy for most Americans. In 1900, an average 65-year-old had a life expectancy of only a few years. In 2001, an average 65-year-old man can expect to live to about age 81. Women can expect to reach about age 84.

If today's retirees have that many years to invest, why shouldn't they take advantage of the higher returns they can get from stocks? The historical record is clear: Over the 73 years from 1926 to 1999, large-company stocks returned an average of 11.36 percent a year, while long-term government bonds returned 5.3 percent a year, according to Ibbotson Associates, a Chicago research firm. By investing in stocks, it appears, retirees can improve their chances of stretching out their retirement dollars.

INFLATION IS NOT YOUR FRIEND

Our new and longer investment horizons mean that retirees have to worry more about inflation than they did before. Inflation has always been a concern for individuals who live on fixed incomes, but before the dramatic increase in life expectancy, there may have been less concern about the effects of inflation on retirees. After all, if your retirement was going to last only for a few years, you didn't have to worry much about inflation. But if your retirement is going to last for 15 or 20 years, inflation can have a substantial impact on the value of your savings.

Although inflation has been subdued in recent years, it averaged 4.6 percent a year during the 22 years between 1977 and 1999, according to the folks at T. Rowe Price. For example, if you retired in 1977 with $20,000 in savings, the impact of inflation would have reduced your purchasing power to $7500 by 1999. That's why today's retirees are advised not to be too conservative in their investments. It may seem safe to put all of one's savings in money market funds, bank CDs, or even government bonds, but your gains can be zapped by inflation.

Your goal as a retiree should be to develop an investment portfolio that provides relative safety, current income for living expenses, and the growth of your savings. How can you do this? The best way is to use a mix of stock, bond, and money market instruments, tailored to your special situation and needs. While stocks suffer from more ups and downs than bonds do, you can reduce the volatility of your stock investments by using conservative mutual funds, such as equity income funds, which invest in high-yielding stocks, and balanced funds, which invest in a mix of stocks and bonds. Research by T. Rowe Price shows that in falling markets these types of funds declined less and came back faster than the overall market.

OUR CHANGING MARKETS

Financial markets have changed dramatically in the last several decades. The 1980s and 1990s saw the rise of the mutual fund industry. Today, there are 7869 mutual funds holding $7 trillion that belongs to you and to me and probably to everybody else we've ever met. The stock market, once a playground for the wealthy few, has become the home field for millions of Americans who invest through mutual funds or buy individual stocks.

The creation of an "everyman's market" has forever changed many of the dynamics of investing. The speculators and day traders will always be with us, of course; indeed, the ease of Internet trading has increased their numbers. But, fortunately, the stock market is still dominated by long-term investors—people who are saving for retirement or saving so that they can buy a new home or send their kids to college. In this respect, the financial markets have become repositories for the dreams of millions of Americans.

A FLOOR UNDER THE MARKETS

The record shows that even when markets tremble and sometimes fall, it is the long-term investors who hang in there, sit tight, and wait for the market to calm down and come back. By and large, these individuals do not panic, nor do they try to sell everything and flee. Indeed, billions of dollars are in pension and retirement plans—and that money is pretty well protected against investor panic.

The presence in the market of millions of long-term, wait-it-out investors means that there are billions of dollars that, in effect, put a floor under the market and give it a solid base of support. That support makes it easier for the market to rebound from occasional minicrashes.

Turning your nest egg into income

Many retirees, I have found, need to use their savings to produce a monthly income that can help close the gap between their income and their monthly living expenses. The question is, What's the best way to accomplish this goal? I took the question to a friend, Jack R. May, a certified financial planner (CFP) at the firm of Lara, Shull, & May, Ltd., in Vienna, Virginia. I met Jack May 15 years ago, when I wanted to develop a better understanding of financial markets, investments, and corporate accounting. At the time, he was teaching financial planning at George Washington University in Washington, D.C. I enrolled in a couple of his courses and learned many valuable things.

I asked May what he would recommend to a person who retires at age 65 with Social Security benefits, a company pension, and $100,000 accumulated over many years in a company 401(k) plan. In this scenario, the retiree has rolled over his money into a tax-deferred IRA account at a brokerage firm or mutual fund company. The retiree's basic goal would be twofold: to get as much income as possible and to preserve his or her nest egg as long as possible by taking only investment income from the $100,000, leaving the principal intact.

One small wrinkle is that at age $70\frac{1}{2}$, as described in Chapter 6, retirees must begin to take money out of their retirement accounts. Of course, there is nothing to prevent a retiree from reinvesting that money in a taxable account, although I have generally used part of the money to pay the taxes due on the withdrawal. Thus, it might be difficult to use the full $100,000 to produce income after age $70\frac{1}{2}$.

How, I asked Jack May, can a 65-year-old retiree use that $100,000 to produce a flow of monthly income that would beat bank savings rates or certificates of deposit? How much income could $100,000 produce? And for how long?

May mulled the idea for a while and said there were four main investment choices: an immediate annuity, a portfolio of Treasury bonds, a growth-stock mutual fund, and a high-yield, or "junk" bond, mutual fund. However, May said, before retirees decide where to invest, they should first decide whether to put the full $100,000 to work generating income or whether to use part of the money for income and invest the rest for growth of principal. "The ultimate objective," May told me, "is to keep pace with inflation, and one way to achieve that is to keep some of your money in a conservative stock fund that will grow over time."

In the past, retirees often were advised to stick to bonds because stocks were too risky for those over 65. But, as mentioned earlier, that view has changed, and many financial advisers suggest that retirees keep at least a portion of their savings in growth stocks or growth funds. Here are the details on Jack May's four choices for a $100,000 investment that produces income:

An immediate annuity

This is a retirement investment sold by insurance companies. In its simplest form, you give your $100,000 to an insurance company, which then pays you a monthly income for life, starting immediately. Depending on the type of payment you choose, the $100,000 could produce as much as $9634 or as little as $8287 a year, or between $803 and $691 a month. These figures are for annuities sold by First Colony Life Insurance Co. of Lynchburg, Virginia, and based on rates as of March 29, 2000.

An annuity gives you several payment options. For instance, you can take the maximum monthly income for as long as you live. But your spouse gets nothing after you die. This single life option would produce $803 a month. That sounds good until you realize that if you invest your $100,000 and live for only two years afterward, the insurance company stops paying and your money is gone.

A better way to go, perhaps, is to ask the company to pay you for as long as you live, but at least for 20 years. That option would give you $710 a month. If you die before the 20 years are up, the remaining years of income would go to your beneficiary.

A third alternative is a plan that pays you for life and then gives your spouse 50 percent of your monthly payment for as long as he or she may live. That would give you $769 a month for life and your spouse half that amount for his or her life.

A fourth alternative is a 100 percent spousal benefit. You receive only $691 a month, but after your death, your spouse would continue to get the same payment.

All these options are called fixed annuities, because the payments are based on fixed interest rates. However, many companies sell variable annuities, which are generally tied to stock funds or other investments that can grow or shrink in value, providing a possible hedge against inflation.

Another possibility is to put your $100,000 into an annuity that allows you to take interest only. At the moment, that option would produce $6000 a year, or $500 a month, based on a 6 percent interest rate. But why would you want to do that? One reason is that you keep control of your $100,000. You can take it out whenever you want. You can leave it to your spouse or to your heirs. If you leave it in, the rate paid will move up and down as interest rates change. Should rates move up sharply, you could convert the interest-only annuity to a fixed payment.

Treasury bond portfolio

The idea here is to use the $100,000 to buy a group of bonds with the dates of their maturity arranged like a "ladder," or in a staggered manner. Taking interest only, this method would produce $6303 a year, or $525.25 a month, as of March 29, 2000.

Jack May suggests putting $25,000 each in two-year bonds (at 6.55 percent), in five-year bonds (at 6.42 percent), in 10-year bonds (at 6.14 percent) and in 20-year bonds (at 6.1 percent). Notice that the rates decline as the term of the bond gets longer. That is the opposite of the normal pattern. The reason is that the Federal Reserve was gradually raising rates in the 1999-2000 period to head off any inflation generated by a booming economy. As a result, investors believe that interest rates in the future will be lower than they are today. And that has caused near-term rates to go higher and long-term rates to go lower, reversing the way interest rates usually behave.

The purpose of "laddering" the portfolio, May said, is to obtain an average of varying interest rates. Also, with groups of bonds coming due at different times, a big chunk of money can become available to the retiree for any special needs, without a forced sale of bonds at market prices.

Growth-stock mutual fund

May said that retirees who are interested in keeping their monthly income flowing can achieve that goal by investing in a blue-chip, growth-stock fund. His idea is based on statistics mentioned earlier in this chapter which show that, over the 73 years from 1926 to 1999, large-company stocks returned an average of 11.36 percent a year, according to Ibbotson Associates. As a result, May said, an investor could take 5 percent of his or her money out of the stock fund each year to use as income and leave the balance in the fund to grow. In the first year, a 5 percent withdrawal would produce $5,000, or $417 a month.

In an effort to be very conservative, May said he assumed that the growth fund would rise at only 8 percent a year. The annual 5 percent withdrawal would thus leave 3 percent for additional growth. That 3 percent left in the fund each year, May said, would enable the fund to grow to $134,392 at the end of 10 years and $180,611 at the end of 20 years. Because of the increase in value of the fund, May said, the income from a 5 percent withdrawal would rise to $6720 in 10 years and to $9031 in 20 years. It's worth remembering, however, that markets do not always go up, and a mutual fund easily could lose 3 percent or more in any given year. However, experience shows that long-term growth generally overcomes short-term volatility.

High-yield bond mutual fund

This type of fund is sometimes known as a "junk bond fund." At current interest rates and on the basis of the returns produced by the Van Kampen Corporate Bond Fund, the fund would produce $10,680 a year, or $757 a month. Van Kampen is a subsidiary of Morgan Stanley Dean Witter. Its fund invests in low-quality, high-yielding corporate bonds. On Wall Street, bond quality ratings start at AAA and go down from there. Anything above BBB is considered an "investment-grade" bond. Anything below BBB is called a "junk bond."

Bonds in the Van Kampen fund have a B rating, on average. Not surprisingly, companies with lower credit or junk bond ratings pay more interest on their bonds to attract investors than do companies with higher credit ratings. Those higher interest payments are what make junk bonds so attractive to investors.

Junk bond funds, like all bond funds, are subject to interest rate risk: As interest rates rise, the value of the fund will fall, and vice versa. That means that a retiree's income could fluctuate as interest rates change. And another risk involving junk bonds is that a company that issues them can get into financial trouble and be unable to pay the interest on its bonds. Defaults do happen from time to time, but many junk bond funds have excellent track records for reviewing and avoiding questionable issues.

Faced with May's four income-producing investment choices, which one would I select? Basically, I would divide the $100,000 between a junk bond fund and the blue-chip, high-dividend growth-stock fund. But remember, when it comes to investment decisions, one size does not fit all. Your financial situation is likely to be different from mine. And your tolerance for risk—otherwise called your ability to sleep at night without worrying about your money—is different, too.

Why would I make these choices? Here are my reasons: The junk bond fund provides the highest current income, with a return of about 10.7 percent today. Getting a high income would be one of my primary goals, and putting $50,000 in this fund would give me $5340 a year, or $445 a month, in income.

But an equally important goal is to seek some growth for our nest egg and thus give ourselves a hedge against inflation. For that, I would turn to a conservative growth-stock mutual fund. Putting $50,000 into the fund and taking out 5 percent a year would give me $2,500 in the first year, or $208 a month in income.

If the stock fund does grow, as anticipated, our 5 percent annual withdrawals would also provide a greater number of dollars in the future. At the outset, however, this dual strategy would give me $7840 for the first year, or $653 a month in income. That beats the Treasury bond portfolio. It also beats the interest-only annuity. It does not beat the four fixed-annuity options. But it would allow us to keep control of our nest egg— and even to pass it on to our heirs— unless, of course, we decide to spend it all first.

For more information

Books

Ellis, Lisa and the editors of *Money* magazine. *The Money Guide to Living Well in Retirement.* Money Books, 1999.

Kehrer, Daniel. *Kiplinger's 12 Steps to a Worry-Free Retirement.* Kiplinger Books, 1993.

The Vanguard Group. *The Vanguard Guide to Investing During Retirement.* New York, McGraw-Hill, 1998.

Financial Planners

You can get a list of certified financial planners (CFPs) in your community from the Financial Planning Association at 1-800-647-6340 or on the organization's Web site at www.fpanet.org. If you phone, the names of several planners in your area will be mailed to you.

Fee-only planners are represented by the National Association of Personal Financial Advisors. To obtain a list of fee-only planners in your home area, call 1-888-333-6659, and a list will be mailed to you. The list also is available at www.napfa.org.

WEB SITES

Many of the nation's mutual funds operate Web sites that offer advice on investment and retirement. Some sites also have retirement "calculators" that will help you figure out how much you need to save for retirement or how long your money will last in retirement.

Some of the major mutual fund Web sites are found at these addresses:

- American Century Investments: www.americancentury.com
- Fidelity Investments: www.fidelity.com
- INVESCO Funds Group: www.invesco.com
- MFS Investment Management: www.mfs.com
- OppenheimerFunds: www.oppenheimerfunds.com
- Putnam Investment Management: www.putnamfunds.com
- T. Rowe Price Associates: www.troweprice.com
- The Vanguard Group: www.vanguard.com

DECISION 8

What should I do about health insurance?

As we journey through retirement, few things are more important to Sara and me than our health insurance. At our ages, 74 and 72, respectively, we are increasingly vulnerable to medical problems and the huge expenses that come with them. Unfortunately, we both know what it's like to need costly medical attention. Shortly before we retired, I had a quadruple heart bypass operation and Sara had surgery for breast cancer. Fortunately, our company health insurance policies paid for most of our hospital and doctor bills. It was a good thing they did: My medical costs totaled about $45,000, and Sara's were more than $20,000. Without our insurance, we'd have been in debt for years.

When Sara and I retired, we lost the health coverage we had at our companies. So we migrated to Medicare, the federal insurance program that pays the hospital and doctors' bills of almost 40 million elderly and disabled Americans. At the same time, we signed up for a secondary insurance policy that was offered by GE, Sara's former employer, as a retirement benefit. The policy, which covers both of us, pays for some of the medical charges not covered by Medicare. If the GE policy had not been available, we would have bought a "medigap" policy. Why?

Basically, because Medicare pays for most—but not all—of our hospital and doctors' bills. There is literally a gap between what hospitals and doctors charge us as patients and what Medicare will pay those providers for their services. Hence, the name "medigap"—for insurance policies that close the "gap" by paying for certain services that Medicare won't pay for. If we didn't have this type of coverage, we would have to pay those costs ourselves—and that could add up to a lot of money over time.

Here's an example of how the Medicare system works when it comes to doctors' bills: Let's say I go to my doctor and she charges me $100 for the visit. The doctor sends the bill to Medicare, which decides that the visit was worth only $80. Thus, $80 becomes what Medicare calls the "approved charge" for that visit. Under federal rules, Medicare pays only 80 percent of an "approved charge."

That means that Medicare will pay the doctor 80 percent of $80, or $64. If you have a medigap policy, it will pay the other 20 percent of the $80, or $16. If you don't have a medigap policy, you may have to pay the $16 yourself.

That is a bare-bones explanation of the way Medicare deals with doctors' bills. There are many other aspects of Medicare that current and future retirees need to know about. The bottom line is that it's a giant government program and can be complicated and even frustrating at times. But if you are a retiree, you can depend on one thing: Medicare will play a major role in the quality and cost of your health care. In order to make the most of Medicare's benefits, you have to understand how the system works.

What is Medicare?

Medicare is a federal health insurance program for people who are age 65 and older. It also covers people who are under 65 with certain disabilities and people who suffer from what is called "end-stage renal disease." The Medicare definition of the latter is "permanent kidney failure treated with dialysis or a transplant." Generally speaking, you can get Medicare if you or your spouse worked for 10 years in Medicare-covered employment. You must also be a citizen or permanent resident of the United States.

There are two parts to the Medicare program.

Medicare Part A

This is the side of Medicare that pays for hospital bills. Most people do not pay for Part A if they have had 40 quarters—equal to 10 years—of Social Security earnings. With at least 30 quarters, they would pay $166 a month. With less than 30 quarters, it would be $301 a month.

In 2000, hospital patients paid a $776 deductible for each hospital stay. They did not pay anything additional for the first 60 days in the hospital. For days 61-90, they paid $194 a day. From days 91-150, they paid $388 a day. Those last 60 days are considered "reserve days." You get a total of 60 lifetime reserve days, which are not renewable.

Medicare Part B

This is the side of Medicare that pays for doctors' bills, medical tests, and related expenses. Most people pay monthly for Part B coverage. In 2000, the monthly charge was $45.50. The payments are deducted from our monthly Social Security benefits.

Medicare payments also are deducted from railroad retirement and civil service retirement checks. There is a $100-a-year deductible.

Medicare pays for many hospital and medical services. Subject to strict limitations, Part A pays for hospital stays, home health care, hospice care, and skilled nursing facility care. Again subject to strict limitations, Part B pays for doctors' services, laboratory tests, outpatient hospital services, medical equipment, and home health care.

But there are also a number of important items that Medicare does not pay for. When my wife and I joined Medicare, we were surprised to discover that it did not pay for dental care, vision exams, eyeglasses (except after cataract surgery), hearing aids and exams, prescription drugs (prescribed on an outpatient basis), routine physical exams, and private nurses.

I wish I had known about all those things before I retired. When Sara and I were working, our company insurance plans covered dental care, routine physicals, and prescription drugs. Once we lost that coverage, it meant that we would have to pick up those expenses ourselves—and items like gold crowns cost $1500 each at our dentist! As a result, our retirement budget should have included a couple of thousand dollars a year for medical, dental, and prescription drug expenses. Keep that in mind when you are drawing up your retirement budget.

Applying for Medicare

Although I didn't retire and go on Medicare Part B until I was 69, I signed up for Medicare Part A when I turned 65. If you continue to work after you reach 65 and continue to have company health insurance, as I did, you should take Part A at 65 and wait on Part B until you retire. And that's fine with the folks at the SSA and Medicare, who want people to sign up when they first become eligible. However, as noted, they make exceptions for people who continue to work after 65.

If, like many people, you decide to retire when you turn 65, it's a good idea to sign up for both Part A and Part B at that time. In fact, notify the SSA three months before you reach 65; that will help ensure that your Medicare coverage will begin when your company insurance is ending.

Don't delay. Delay could cost you money. If you wait 12 months or more to sign up for Medicare, your monthly premiums will go up. Part B premiums will rise 10 percent for each 12 months that you could have enrolled but didn't. The increase in the Part A premium—if you have to pay a premium—will be 10 percent no matter how late you are. To enroll in Medicare, call the SSA number, 1-800-772-1213.

Choosing a medigap policy

We come now to the ins and outs of choosing a medigap policy, which, as I've mentioned, is intended to fill the gap between what your medical expenses are and what Medicare pays. At this point, it won't surprise you to learn that choosing a medigap policy is a decision that can be rather complicated.

Some years ago, the federal government decided to standardize the various types of medigap policies (also called "Medicare supplemental insurance" policies). So, in most states, insurance companies are permitted to sell only 10 standard medigap policies. These policies are lettered A through J, as shown in Table 8.1. In each letter group, all policies must have the same benefits, no matter which insurance company issues the policy. But remember, medigap policies will pay only for items that Medicare covers. If Medicare won't pay for a medical procedure, neither will a medigap policy.

Moreover, bear in mind that not all companies sell all 10 policies and not all policies are sold in all 50 states. You can only buy a plan that is approved by regulators in your state. And, by the way, it is illegal for an insurance company to sell a medigap policy to a person who already has one.

With medigap insurance, like most other things in life, you get what you pay for. The United Seniors Health Cooperative of Washington, D.C., recently analyzed the 10 standard medigap policies and concluded that Plan A was the cheapest and offered the fewest benefits, while Plan J was the most expensive and offered the best benefits.

Limited coverage for prescription drugs is available in Plans H, I, and J. However, prescription coverage has significant restrictions, as United Seniors points out. The most any plan will pay is 50 percent, after a yearly deductible and with an annual limit. Even under Plan J, your prescription costs would need to exceed $6250 each year for you to get the maximum benefit.

If you are shopping for medigap insurance and you hear the phrase "Medicare Select," you should know that *any* medigap policy may be sold as a "Medicare Select" policy. Medicare Select policies often cost less than similar policies because they require you to use certain hospitals and doctors. However, in an emergency, you may use any doctor or hospital.

United Seniors has drawn up a number of suggestions on how to shop for medigap insurance. The most important thing is to

TABLE 8.1 Medigap Benefits, by Plan

Medigap Benefits	A	B	C	D	E	F	G	H	I	J
Basic Benefits	√	√	√	√	√	√	√	√	√	√
Part A: Hospital Deductible		√	√	√	√	√	√	√	√	√
Part A: Skilled-Nursing Home Coinsurance (days 21–100)			√	√	√	√	√	√	√	√
Part B: Deductible			√			√				√
Foreign Travel Emergency			√	√	√	√	√	√	√	√
At-Home Recovery				√			√		√	√
Part B: Excess Doctor Charges						100%	80%		100%	100%
Preventive Screening					√					√
Outpatient Prescription Drugs								Basic	Basic	Extended

Note: Plans F and J also have a high-deductible option. If you choose this option, you must pay $1500 a year out of pocket before the plans pay anything. An insurance policy with a high deductible generally costs less than a policy with a lower deductible.

Source: United Seniors Health Cooperative.

compare premiums, because there are great variations in the premiums different companies charge for exactly the same coverage. In evaluating premiums, be sure you are comparing identical plans. One key to price shopping is to understand that companies use three different methods to calculate annual premiums:

Issue age

The premium is set when you buy the policy. You continue to pay the premium required of a person of the same age you were when the policy was issued. For example, if you buy a policy at age 65, you will always pay the rate the company charges people who are 65, regardless of your advancing age. However, the rate for 65-year-olds could go up.

Attained age

The premium is based upon your current age and increases automatically as you grow older. Typically, these plans will be less expensive at younger ages, but they may cost considerably more in later years. The vast majority of policies sold in this country are based on attained age.

No age rating

A few companies charge the same premium for all policyholders, regardless of age. These policies may be more expensive initially, but less expensive in the long run. For people over age 75, a policy with no age rating may be less costly than one based on attained age. You should compare policies on the basis of what they are likely to cost you over the next 5 or 10 years. Be alert for discounts that some policies make available to couples or nonsmokers.

There is one other important difference among medigap insurers. Some companies may ask you to take a physical exam when applying for a medigap policy. This approach is called "medical underwriting." Other companies sell policies on a "guaranteed issue" basis; that is, they do *not* ask you to take a physical. But their policies may be more costly than those of companies that insist on physical exams. If you are in good health and can easily pass a physical, it may be less expensive to go with a company that requires a medical exam.

The preceding ideas generally apply to policies lettered A through G. Policies H, I, and J have prescription drug benefits attached, so medigap insurers may have somewhat different rules for those policies. Note that all of this assumes that you are not covered by an open enrollment period, which will be is described shortly.

What does medigap cost?

When it comes to medigap policies, it pays to shop around. Prices vary widely for policies that provide the same coverage. So where can you get a list of insurance companies that sell medigap policies and of the prices of those policies?

A good place to start is with the state insurance department in the state in which you live. An insurance company cannot sell you a medigap policy unless it has been approved for sale in your state. Thus, state insurance departments are likely to be able to provide you with information about companies that sell medigap policies in your state and about the prices of those policies.

The Maryland Insurance Administration, for instance, has a list of companies which sell medigap policies in that state and of the prices they charge for policies A through J. The list shows that A-level policies sell for as little as $368, and as much as $890, a year. The list also shows that F-level policies have a range from

$747 on the low side to $1730 on the high side. Finally, relatively few companies sell the top-rated J policies, which offer limited prescription coverage. At the J level, the price range is from $2032 on the low end to $4164 on the high end.

Nationally, prices vary from state to state, and, as mentioned, not all companies sell all policies in all states. An April 2000 national survey by Weiss Ratings, Inc., of Palm Beach Gardens, Florida, showed that, among companies using attained-age standards, A-level policies sold for as little as $336 and as much as $1627. At the F level, the lowest price was $684, the highest $2048. The highest H-level policy was $9681, the lowest $960. Given these wide variations in price, it is obviously important to shop around and carefully compare the costs of medigap policies that are available in your state.

Don't miss the open-enrollment period

One of the most important things for future retirees to know is that there is a one-time open-enrollment period for buying medigap insurance. What does this mean? It means that during this period, insurance companies are prohibited from denying medigap coverage to Medicare beneficiaries for health or other reasons. The period lasts six months.

Medicare explains it this way: "For six months after the first day of the month in which you are age 65 or older and join Medicare Part B, you have the right to buy the medigap policy of your choice.

"During this open enrollment period, the insurance company cannot deny you insurance coverage or change the price of a policy because of past or current health problems. Once you enroll in Part B, the six month medigap open enrollment period starts and cannot be changed."

For people who work after age 65 and for younger people who receive Medicare, there are special open-enrollment rules.

Joining a Medicare HMO

Shortly after I retired and signed up for Social Security and Medicare—what is now called "original Medicare"—I began to get mail from health maintenance organizations, or HMOs. Almost every day, there would be another postcard, letter, or brochure in my mailbox touting the advantages of joining an HMO designed for people on Medicare. The HMOs made the idea sound very enticing. They said they could offer me the same health coverage that Medicare gives me, plus dental, vision, hearing, and prescription benefits, items not covered by Medicare. And, they said, I could get all of this coverage without paying additional insurance premiums. I'd continue to pay my monthly Medicare Part B coverage fee, which would continue to be deducted from my monthly Social Security check. I also would pay the HMO $5 or $10 for doctors' visits, along with a few other small copayments. But, basically, the HMOs said, life in an HMO wouldn't cost me more than in original Medicare. In fact, it could save me money in the long run.

The marketing literature made it plain that if my wife and I joined a Medicare HMO, we could give up our secondary insurance policy. We just wouldn't need it. That sounded good, because if we dropped our policy, we would save $100 a month, or $1200 a year. But as appealing as the HMO offers sounded, Sara and I soon realized that, for us, there was an important downside to the idea. The problem was that when you join an HMO, you are locked into using its physicians and its medical providers. That, I am sure, works well for many people, but we didn't think it would work for us.

Under our original Medicare program, run on a fee-for-service basis, Sara and I are free to choose our own doctors, hospitals, and other medical providers. If we were to join an HMO, we would give up that freedom. It might mean that we would have to switch doctors, something we were not keen to do. Also, we weren't sure we wanted to have a "gatekeeper." In HMOs, your primary-care physician serves as the person who refers you to specialists, and you generally can't see a specialist without a referral.

So before you join a Medicare HMO, ask about the HMO's policies regarding referrals and whether the HMO has been sued for refusing to grant referrals. It's also a good idea to ask an HMO about its patient turnover, which may indicate whether the HMO has a large number of unhappy members.

Many seniors join Medicare HMOs because they want to get the extra coverage for routine physical, vision, hearing, and dental exams and the discounts on dental work, eyeglasses, and hearing aids. Perhaps, more importantly, they want coverage for prescription drugs. Indeed, the need for drug coverage is uppermost in the minds of the seniors who regularly come in contact with Leta S. Blank, coordinator for the Senior Health Insurance Assistance Program (SHIP) in Montgomery County, Maryland. "The biggest issue facing seniors is the cost of prescription drugs, which are not covered under Medicare or most medigap policies," Blank told me. As a result, she said, prescription coverage has become "one of the most attractive features for joining an HMO."

However, she noted that in the last few years some companies that operate Medicare HMOs have tightened up on the amount of prescription drugs that they will pay for each year. Some HMOs also have increased copayments. And, of course, remember that in some regions of the country Medicare HMOs simply quit the business when they felt that those regions were not sufficiently profitable. That left members of those HMOs in a difficult situation, forcing them to try to find another HMO or go back to original Medicare.

As it turned out, it was probably a good thing that Sara and I did not leave original Medicare for a Medicare HMO. Several of the HMOs that were serving our region later decided to leave the area, and their members had to move to another Medicare HMO or go back to original Medicare. We easily could have been members of one of the Medicare HMOs that closed.

In those situations, it can sometimes be difficult to get back the medigap policy you gave up when you joined the HMO. Or even if you can get medigap coverage, it may not be the policy you want. However, Medicare points out that there are at least three limited situations in which people who have joined Medicare HMOs may be able to get new medigap policies or retrieve the ones they had before they joined the HMO:

- You can get your medigap policy back if you lost your health coverage through no fault of your own, as when the HMO quits the business.
- You can get your policy back if you joined an HMO for the first time, but decided to leave within a year.
- If you were new to Medicare when you joined an HMO and thus did not have a medigap policy, you can probably get any policy you want if you decide to leave the HMO within a year.
- To get those protections, you have to apply for a medigap policy within 63 calendar days after your previous coverage ends. To see how the rules may apply to you, call 1-800-633-4227, and talk to a Medicare customer service representative.

Pushing the frontiers of Medicare

In 2000, about 40 million people were receiving Medicare benefits. The vast majority, about 83 percent, were enrolled in the original Medicare program. Of the 40 million, an estimated 6.2 million people, or about 15.5 percent, were enrolled in Medicare HMOs. Another 700,000 were enrolled in other types of Medicare plans. The figures came from the federal Health Care Financing Administration (HCFA), the agency that ran Medicare. The agency has been renamed The Centers for Medicare & Medicaid Services (CMMS).

Clearly, for the last decade it has been the policy of the federal government to encourage the creation and use of Medicare HMOs and other forms of managed care in the hope of saving money.

However, as of the summer of 2000, the government was not making much headway toward that objective.

In the Balanced Budget Act of 1997, in an effort to reduce Medicare spending, Congress cut $116 billion from the program over five years, some of which it later put back under pressure from doctors, nurses, hospitals, medical schools, and home care advocates. But the act also established a new program called Medicare Plus Choice, intended to give Medicare beneficiaries a wider selection of managed care and insurance-related options.

When the Medicare Plus Choice program was published in late 1998, this was the lineup of choices that Medicare hoped would be offered to its beneficiaries:

Original Medicare

This basic fee-for-service plan provides hospital insurance (Part A) and medical insurance (Part B). Medicare enrollees, who paid $45.50 a month to the program for the Part B premium in 2000, are free to choose almost any doctor or hospital they want. Medicare pays its share of the approved charges, often 80 percent, and the patient pays the rest. Medigap policies generally cover the portion not covered by Medicare.

Medicare Health Maintenance Organizations (HMOs)

If you join a Medicare HMO, you will continue to pay Medicare your $45.50-a-month premium. Medicare in turn will pay your HMO a specific sum for your health care, based on geographic and medical considerations. HMOs require their members to use doctors and hospitals in the HMO networks. Some HMOs offer prescription, hearing, vision, dental, and other benefits not covered by Medicare. Some HMOs charge monthly premiums, while others do not charge at all. Charges for office visits and other fees tend to be low, but if you go outside the network, you'll have to pay the bill yourself. If your HMO has a point-of-service option, it may cover part of out-of-network costs.

Provider-Sponsored Organizations (PSOs)

A PSO can be created by a group of doctors or hospitals that decides to take on the financial risk of setting up a medical care business. A PSO resembles a Medicare HMO. Here again, you continue to pay your Part B premium to Medicare, which in turn pays the PSO for your care. Your PSO may charge a monthly premium and small per-visit fees. PSOs may be most popular in rural areas where there aren't enough people to attract the HMOs sponsored by large insurance companies.

Preferred-Provider Organizations (PPOs)

A Medicare PPO may have a broader network of doctors and hospitals than an HMO. As in an HMO, however, you pay your Part B premium to Medicare, which then pays the PPO for your care. Unlike HMOs, however, PPOs do not require their members to use the network's providers. But if you go outside the network, the PPO will pay only part of the bill.

Private Fee-for-Service Plans (PFFSs)

To use this plan, you select a private insurance plan that accepts Medicare beneficiaries. You continue to pay your Part B premium. In turn, Medicare pays the private plan for your coverage. You may go to any doctor or hospital of your choice. The plan may offer benefits not offered by Medicare, but it may require you to pay premiums, deductibles, or coinsurance.

Medicare Medical Savings Accounts (MSAs)

The concept of the MSA goes something like this: Medicare would set aside the amount of money it expects to spend on your health care each year. You would buy a health insurance policy with a high annual deductible—up to $6000—from a private insurance company. Medicare would pay the monthly premium for your policy. Then, to pay medical bills, you would set up a special MSA savings account that could be applied to the deductible. Each January, HCFA would deposit a lump sum in your account. How much? It would deposit the difference between the amount the agency puts aside for your health care and the cost of your high-deductible policy. If your medical bills eat up all the money in your MSA account, you might have to pay out of pocket until you reach the deductible. Then the insurance policy would begin to pay your bills.

Two types of Medicare MSA plans may be offered: a network plan that requires beneficiaries to use doctors in the network, and a nonnetwork plan that allows you to see any doctor you wish. Enrollment in MSAs will take place once a year for a one-year period. The MSA will be renewed automatically, unless you decide to quit during the enrollment period. If you do, money left in the account can be used for future medical bills. If you stay healthy, the money in the account can accumulate and draw interest. If used for medical bills, it will not be taxed. But if you use it for nonmedical items, it will be taxed as income. If you become seriously ill, it may be costly to meet the high deductible.

People who seek coverage from a managed care plan will find new rules for changing plans. Currently, you can change your plan once a month, but that rule will be revised in stages. After January 1, 2002, enrollees will have to wait for an annual open-enrollment period to switch.

The wheels grind slowly

When the new Medicare Plus Choices were unveiled in 1998, HCFA adopted this slogan: "If you're happy with the way you receive your Medicare benefits now, you don't have to do anything." At the time, the idea was that millions of Medicare enrollees would be faced with choosing among the six Medicare Plus Choice options for their medical care. The expectation turned out to be wildly optimistic.

After the new Medicare program was announced, it was up to the insurance companies that conducted business in the managed care arena to offer the health coverage that would make the new Medicare choices a reality. But two years later, in mid-2000, there still weren't many companies rushing to apply for approval from Medicare to offer the new options.

The creation, approval, and operation of a managed care plan, in almost any form, involves a wealth of factors. Insurance companies understandably are reluctant to enter a business unless they feel sure that they can earn a reasonable profit. Whether they can may depend on the HCFA ground rules that they have to observe. Meanwhile, HCFA's primary goal is to protect the interests of Medicare beneficiaries by making sure that managed care companies provide dependable service at what HCFA considers to be a reasonable cost. Between these two goals are scores of legal, ethical, and technical issues that must be resolved if the Medicare Plus Choice options are to see the light of day. And that could take lots of time.

The future of Medicare

In the summer of 2000, the nation's policymakers were wrestling with the highly complex and difficult question of how to reform and strengthen the Medicare program so that it could meet the challenges presented by the 77 million baby boomers who will begin to retire in 2010.

To get a glimpse of the challenge, take a look at these facts:

- In 2000, there were 35 million Americans who were 65 or older. In 2025, there will be 62 million Americans 65 or older. Simply put, by 2025, there will be an additional 27 million people on Medicare. And the rest of the 77 million baby boomers will be moving toward retirement age—and Medicare eligibility.
- While the demand for Medicare funds will be exploding, the resources of the program will be shrinking. The Hospital Insurance Trust Fund, which pays for inpatient hospital expenses under Part A of Medicare, will be able to pay full benefits only until 2023, just 13 years after the baby boomers begin to retire. Then the fund will be in financial trouble unless the policymakers in Washington, D.C., find a way to fix the problem.
- The other side of Medicare won't be much better off. The Supplementary Medical Insurance Trust Fund, which pays doctor bills under Part B of the program, is adequately financed into the indefinite future only because current law requires its annual funding to be based on next year's expected costs. However, that simply means that Congress must keep putting up more and more money. Costs increased 38 percent from 1994 to 1999 and can be expected to keep rising.
- The overall health care situation will not be helped by the fact that health care coverage for retirees is being provided by fewer and fewer business organizations. Nationally, only 22 percent of firms offered health insurance to retirees 65 or older in 1998, and the percentage has been dropping each year.

- One of the major national health care issues centers on whether to create a prescription drug benefit for Medicare recipients. The debate involves many divisive questions, including this one: Should prescription drug coverage be granted to all Medicare beneficiaries or only to persons with low incomes?

- Although the costs of addressing the prescription drug issue are large, the need is real. Modern medicines play a significant role in keeping people healthy and out of hospitals. Yet some of these new medications are so costly that many of the elderly persons who need them cannot afford them. Policymakers in the nation's capital will find it difficult to ignore the needs of these people, and in the long run they will have to come up with an answer.

For more information

WEB SITES

The official Medicare Web site, www.medicare.gov, contains basic information and allows you to compare the costs and features of health insurance policies and nursing homes. The Web site of the Centers for Medicare & Medicaid Services, the federal agency that runs Medicare, is www.cms.hhs.gov It contains information about various organizational and policy matters related to health care.

TELEPHONE NUMBERS

Call 1-800-MEDICARE (1-800-633-4227) for information and publications.

PUBLICATIONS

Medicare publishes more than two dozen booklets. The most useful ones are as follows:

- *Guide to Choosing a Nursing Home*
- *Guide to Health Insurance*; also comes in a large-print version.
- *Medicare & You 2000*; also comes in a large-print version.
- *Medicare Supplemental Insurance (Medigap) Policies and Protections*

What should I do to prepare for serious illness?

I don't know what scares you about growing older, but I can tell you what scares me. It's the idea that my health or the health of my wife, Sara, might deteriorate to the point where one of us would have to become a resident of a nursing home for an extended period of time. What really frightens me isn't just the prospect of illness and the regimentation of nursing home life, but the very real threat that we could be wiped out financially by the cost of that care.

The national average fee for nursing home care is a whopping $56,000 a year. The figure is based on 1998 data, according to the Health Care Financing Agency (HCFA), which runs the Medicare and Medicaid programs. In the Washington, D.C., area, where I live, nursing homes cost even more—an average of $160 a day, or $58,400 a year, according to Maryland health insurance counselor Leta S. Blank. At those prices, most of the people I know wouldn't be able to pay for nursing home care for very long. I know we wouldn't.

But what happens if you are so ill you have to stay in a nursing home indefinitely? It's no secret. Inevitably, you go on Medicaid, a medical program for the poor, which allows you to remain in a nursing home without paying. But to become eligible for Medicaid, you have to pay the nursing home until you virtually run out of money. It's called "spending down," and as I found out a few years ago when my mother went through the process, it is a distasteful experience, especially because my mother had been careful with money all of her life, always paid her own way, and cherished her independence.

That unhappy experience led Sara and me to sign up for long-term care insurance, also called nursing home insurance, when *The Washington Post* offered it to its employees and spouses a few years ago. The group policy was issued by CNA Insurance Cos. In retirement, I continue to pay for our policies. Naturally, I hope we will never have a reason to use them. When we bought the policies, we were hoping that if we ever had to live in a nursing home, the insurance payments would ease the bite of the nursing home bills, protect us from being wiped out financially, and keep us off the Medicaid rolls. We still feel that way.

Buying a long-term-care policy

The group policy that Sara and I bought from CNA through the *Post* pays $110 a day for nursing home care and $55 a day for home care, with a maximum total benefit of $220,000 each, which equates to 5.5 years in a nursing home. My policy, which I took out at the age of 64, costs $1089.48 a year. Sara's policy, which she took out at the age of 62, costs $945.96 a year. Total: $2035.44 a year. That may seem like a lot of money, but the fact is that the $2035 yearly bill for our group policy is relatively cheap when you look at the price of many individual policies being sold today.

Buying a long-term care policy is a lot like buying a car. The more bells and whistles you want, the more it costs. You can get a policy that pays $100, $150, or even $200 a day for nursing home care. As the benefits go up, so does the cost of the policy, and ditto for home care benefits.

Frankly, I didn't do a lot of research on the *Post*'s CNA policy when I bought it nine years ago. I wish I had. I might have shopped around for an individual policy that would have given Sara and me more financial protection than we get from the *Post*'s group policy, although it probably would have cost us much more money. If you're interested in long-term care, remember that the younger you are when you buy a policy, the less it will cost per year.

After I retired, I did some research on long-term care policies. The more I look at the provisions of my policy, the more things there are that I wish I could change. For instance, we do not have inflation protection. Without it, we will still be getting a $110-a-day benefit when nursing homes costs will have gone up to $200 or $250 a day.

There are other aspects of my policy that I dislike, including the following:

The waiting period

The policy has a 60-day waiting period for nursing home benefits and a 15-day wait for home care benefits. That means that if I have to go to a nursing home, I would have to pay for the first 60 days myself. At $160 a day, that would be $9600. That's a pretty big deductible.

Waiving the premium

The insurance company says that if I go to a nursing home, I can stop paying the premiums on my long-term care policy. That sounds generous, but wait—that benefit also doesn't kick in until I've been in a nursing home for 60 days. So I'm spending $9600 and still paying my premiums during that 60 days.

Getting paid

To collect under my policy, I would need to show that I have a "qualifying impairment," meaning that I am unable to perform by myself at least two of the so-called activities of daily living. These activities include eating, dressing, going to the toilet, bathing, moving from the bed to the chair, and managing medications.

Who decides whether I can or can't do these things? The insurance company—who else? The policy says that the company will consult with my doctors and caregivers, but it's free to have its own doctor examine me to see whether I have a "qualifying impairment."

Higher rates

The policy says the company can't raise my individual premium, but it can raise the rate of everybody in my class—that is to say, everybody who is my age and who bought the same policy when I did years ago. Thus far, our rates have stayed about the same. But rates do go up from time to time at various companies. And I'm not sure how much more I am prepared to pay.

One other thing that our policy lacks is any sort of "nonforfeiture" clause. The clause comes into effect if you stop paying your premiums after paying them for a specified number of years. It assures you that you will still receive a portion of your long-term care benefits.

While my CNA policy has the aforementioned negatives, it also has some relatively attractive features, including the following:

Home health care

The insurer will pay for home health care services from a variety of therapists, registered or licensed nurses, home health care aides, or medical social workers. Better yet, the insurer also will pay for "homemaker services, such as cooking, cleaning, laundering, organizing bills for payment, and running errands." There is, however, one small catch: A person you hire to provide home health care services must be a registered or licensed nurse or an aide who works for an organization that is licensed, registered, or accredited by either state or professional organizations.

Alternate plan of care

My policy provides that, if I need them, the company will pay for special treatments and devices if the doctors and the insurer agree that they would be medically beneficial.

What do long-term-care policies cost?

The cost of a long-term-care policy depends on several factors: your age, your health, and the features included in the policy. A survey by the Health Insurance Association of America (HIAA) gives us an idea of the average costs for long-term-care policies in 1998. The prices cited are for a base policy, which includes $100 a day for nursing home care, at least $80 a day for an assisted-living facility, and at least $50 a day for home care. The base policy also includes four years of coverage and a 20-day elimination or waiting period.

The HIAA data in Table 9.1 show us what happens to the price of a base policy when you add two important features: a 5 percent annualized inflation protection clause and a nonforfeiture benefit. At age 50, the base policy costs $385; with the two extra features, the cost rises to $1110. At age 65, the base policy costs $1007. With the extra features, it goes up to $2305. In fact, for each age group, adding those two features to a base policy causes the cost of the policy to just about double.

The HIAA study compares the cost of long-term-care policies for participants of different ages. But there are also other ways for consumers to look at long-term-care insurance costs. A study by Weiss Ratings, Inc., of Palm Beach Gardens, Florida, which is an independent provider of insurance company ratings and analysis, compared the prices that are charged by 30 long-term-care insurers for similar policies. About 120 companies sell long-term-care insurance.

TABLE 9.1   Cost of Long-Term-Care Policies

Age	Base	With 5% Compounded Inflation Protection (IP)	With a Nonforfeiture Benefit (NFB)	With IP and NFB
40	$274	$595	$357	$770
50	$385	$888	$485	$1110
65	$1007	$1850	$1232	$2305
79	$4100	$5880	$4779	$7022

Source: Health Insurance Association of America.

The Weiss Ratings study, published in April 2000, showed that nearly identical policies offered to 65-year-olds can vary widely in price. For instance, the most expensive policy, without inflation protection, cost $1366.60 a year, while the least expensive, also without inflation protection, cost $834 a year. Adding inflation protection, of course, caused the prices to jump. For instance, the Pyramid Life Comprehensive Long Term Care Policy cost $1313.20 without inflation protection. When inflation protection was added, the cost rose to $2859.50, an increase of almost 118 percent.

Other factors that influence the cost of long-term-care insurance include the age at which you take out the policy and whether you are buying an individual policy or whether you and your spouse are both buying policies. According to the Weiss study, spousal discounts can save a couple between 7.5 percent and 21 percent of the cost of two single premiums. The Weiss study also shows that the cost of long-term-care coverage rises rapidly after age 60. For example, the average cost of a comprehensive policy at age 60 would be $1169. But the same policy at age 65 would cost $1704, about 46 percent more.

Martin Weiss, the chairman of Weiss Ratings, advises consumers to wait until they are at least age 60 before buying a policy—unless they have a specific medical condition. "If you buy a policy earlier, you could wind up paying many years of premiums on a plan that could be obsolete by the time you need it," he says. "But don't wait too long after age 60 either. If you do," Weiss adds, "You could be charged prohibitively high annual premiums, especially if you have a preexisting health condition."

My perfect policy

If I could design my own policy, it would include these features:

- $150 a day in nursing home benefits
- $120 a day for home care

- Inflation protection of 5 percent compounded annually
- A 20-day waiting period and a 20-day waiver-of-premium period
- A spousal discount (which some companies give to married couples)
- A nonforfeiture benefit
- A maximum $219,000-per-person lifetime benefit (equivalent to four years in a nursing home)
- A shared-care option, which would allow Sara and me to draw from a total pot of $438,000.

When I checked on the approximate cost of that type of policy several years ago, I was told it would cost me about $4600 a year. It was a good policy, but it was also more than I thought I could afford at the time. Inevitably, if you are in the market for a long-term-care policy, you may find yourself forced to compromise between the benefits you want and the coverage you can afford.

Who needs long-term-care insurance?

That brings us to a basic question about long-term-care insurance: How do you decide whether to buy a policy? The answer, I find, depends on your financial and family situations.

Let's talk first about your family situation. If you become seriously ill and have a spouse or child who would be willing or able to be an active caregiver, you may have a good chance to remain at home instead of going to a nursing home. Thus, you may not need nursing home benefits, although a policy providing home health benefits might be useful. However, there is no guarantee that your spouse or children, devoted as they might be, could care for you for very long. When people develop Alzheimer's disease or some other serious medical problems, there may be no choice but to seek the 24-hour care available in a nursing home.

What about the financial issues? Health insurance counselor Leta Blank says individuals should buy a long-term-care policy only if their annual retirement incomes are over $30,000 and if they have assets of $100,000 to $500,000, not including their home or car. Blank also warns, "Buy long-term-care insurance only if you can afford it without making a lifestyle change and if you have the ability to afford a 20 percent to 50 percent increase in premiums in future years."

I discussed these questions with another expert on long-term-care insurance, Priscilla Itscoitz, a specialist in long-term care at AARP in Washington, D.C. "The decision to purchase long-term-care insurance," she told me, "hinges on several related financial questions. First," Itscoitz said, "can you afford long-term-care insurance, and will you be able to pay the premiums over the long run? Second, do your assets amount to enough to warrant protecting them with long-term-care insurance? Third, do you want to avoid becoming a burden on your family? And fourth, do you want to retain as much control as possible over your health care?" If you can answer "yes" to all these questions, Itscoitz said, then you may want to consider purchasing a long-term-care policy.

But what are the chances that you will ever go to a nursing home or, if you do enter a nursing home, that you will spend much time there? According to AARP, research suggests that about half of today's older people will spend some time in a nursing home—from as little as a few weeks to as much as five years. AARP cites several factors that could increase your chances of going to a nursing home:

- You live alone or have no relatives who could care for you at home.
- Your family members tend to live into their eighties or older.
- Your family has a history of heart problems, high blood pressure, diabetes, or some other serious or chronic health problems.

· Your family has a history of stroke or Alzheimer's or Parkinson's disease.

If, after considering all these factors, you decide to buy a long-term-care policy, be prepared to do some hard work to get the right policy from the right company. You'll certainly need to shop around, which means interviewing salespeople from several companies and being steadfast in your refusal to sign anything until you've completed your comparisons. Do not buy any policy that you don't completely understand. Itscoitz notes that people who buy policies get a 30-day "free look." And she said, "If you are unsure or uneasy, return the policy for a full refund."

Beyond the nursing home: other options

Until a few years ago, the nursing home was about the only place in town where you could place an elderly parent or spouse who was no longer physically or mentally able to live in his or her own home. That situation has changed dramatically: Today, in most areas of the country, there are many more options, including group homes, assisted-living facilities, and continuing-care retirement communities. The growth of these facilities has been prompted by the recognition by both nonprofit organizations and entrepreneurs that there is a serious and growing demand for services for the elderly. In addition, many people reaching their sixties and seventies want to prepare for the day when they can no longer live independently.

It is also clear that not all elderly people need a nursing home with its skilled 24-hour care or even its long-term custodial care. Instead, many people can get by with help just in preparing meals, dressing, bathing, or some of the other activities of daily living. American entrepreneurs, always quick to spot a business opportunity, foresaw that as the U.S. population grew older, millions of elderly persons would need that kind of help. Thus was born a new assisted-living industry. Currently, about 1 million Americans live in approximately 20,000 assisted-living facilities, according to the Assisted Living Federation of America.

The trend also has resulted in the creation of thousands of continuing-care retirement communities—often called CCRCs—where you can move in while you are still in good health, and later, if your health deteriorates, you can move to higher levels of care until, finally, you reach the nursing home level. One word of caution about CCRCs, though: Be prepared for a case of "sticker shock" when you see the cost of some of these facilities.

If Sara or I became ill, we would first try to care for each other at home if possible. But as I said before, we would not expect our children to be caregivers. They have their own homes, families, and busy, demanding jobs. While they would be sympathetic and helpful, we'd prefer to organize our own care.

If necessary, we'd hire a home health care aide. Charges vary around the country, but in the Washington, D.C., area, home health agencies charge an average of $12 to $18 an hour for an eight-hour shift, or from $96 to $144 a day, according to area agencies. Charges depend on the number of hours worked and whether evenings or weekends are involved. Agencies generally have a four-hour minimum.

For these expenses, we would get some help from our *Washington Post*–CNA long-term-care insurance policy, which would pay $55 a day for home care, or about half the cost. But if home care didn't meet our needs, we might have to go to a group home or assisted living facility. These establishments are intended for people who can't live on their own, but don't need nursing home care either.

Finding the right assisted-living facility at the right price can be difficult. Nationally, large facilities cost an average of $3000 a month. Smaller group homes may cost $2000 to $2500 a month, but may lack some of the amenities or services of the larger homes; for instance, they may not be able to handle Alzheimer's or dementia cases.

A 1998 study, *Assisted Living for the Frail Elderly*, conducted under contract between the U.S. Department of Health and Human Services and the Research Triangle Institute, reported,

> Assisted living was largely not affordable for moderate and low-income persons aged 75 or older unless they disposed of their assets and spent them down to supplement their income. Further, to the degree that some assisted living facilities were affordable for low- and moderate-income older persons, they were more likely to be assisted living facilities categorized as low-minimal service/low minimal privacy.

The problems of the assisted-living industry are familiar to the Consumer Consortium on Assisted Living. Based in Arlington, Virginia, the CCAL is a national nonprofit organization that provides information and help to consumers on topics and issues associated with assisted living.

I talked with Karen Love, co-chair and acting executive director of the Consumer Consortium's board, about the growth and challenges facing the assisted living industry. "The assisted living industry has grown phenomenally," she told me. "There are currently 1 million residents living in assisted living. Compare this to the estimated 1.5 million nursing home residents, an industry that has been around significantly longer than assisted living, and one understands the explosive growth experienced in assisted living.

"At times," she said, "the growth of assisted living has been at the cost of inferior resident care as quality resident services have not kept pace with the 'bricks and mortar' construction."

"In the year 2000 and beyond," Love continued, "there are two major challenges facing the assisted living industry: developing options to make assisted living affordable to 'middle America'; and instituting a consumer-supported approach to defining quality standards. While baby boomers have been the driving force behind finding alternative means of long-term care, other than nursing homes, they will also have to be the driving force behind demanding quality care and services to support the often physically frail and cognitively impaired resident population of assisted living.

"Affordability will be challenging as well, since there is a limit to how low provider costs can go, thereby limiting how low monthly fees can go. A handful of innovative approaches to help extend affordability beyond the current scope are at development," Love concluded.

The continuing-care option

Perhaps the most attractive option at our stage of life is a continuing-care retirement community, called a CCRC for short. A CCRC provides both housing and access to health care at three levels:

- *Independent living.* You live in your own cottage or apartment for as long as you are physically and mentally able to.
- *Assisted living.* If, as time passes, you require help with dressing, bathing, eating, or any other activities, you can move to the assisted-living area or receive the services you need in your home.
- *Nursing home care.* If you require skilled nursing care, you can move to the nursing home unit, which is part of your CCRC.

An estimated 625,000 Americans now live in more than 2100 CCRCs, according to the American Association of Homes and Services for the Aging in Washington, D.C. (The association gives a seal of approval to CCRCs that meet its rigorous standards.)

To get a sense of what a CCRC is like, Sara and I visited the pastoral 130-acre Asbury Methodist Village in Gaithersburg, Maryland. We talked with John A. Capasso, vice president of health services, development, and integration for Asbury Services, Inc., and several other Asbury administrators.

Asbury Services, a nonprofit corporation, supports several Asbury charitable subsidiaries: the Methodist Village campus in

Gaithersburg, a smaller facility at Solomons Island, Maryland; Bethany Village in Mechanicsburg, Pennsylvania; Epworth Manor in Tyrone, Pennsylvania; and the Asbury Foundation, a fund-raising unit.

Asbury Methodist Village, founded in 1926 as a home for Methodists who are retired, has grown into a community with 1400 residents. Asbury is open to all, regardless of sex, creed, color, religion, or national origin.

Like many CCRCs, Asbury gives its residents a sense of security because they know that if they become ill temporarily or need long-term care as they age, it will be available in familiar surroundings. Asbury managers, moreover, provide residents with opportunities for an active physical and intellectual life. Residents can take part in a variety of programs and use the community's recreational facilities. Sara and I liked the CCRC concept and were favorably impressed by the caring attitude we saw at Asbury.

Asbury and most other CCRCs require both entry fees and monthly fees. If we wanted to move to Asbury, the managers would study our financial assets and monthly incomes to see whether we could afford to live there for an extended period of time. Our costs would depend largely on the kind of housing we selected. To move there, we'd first have to sign a contract that spells out the details of what we'd pay and what we'd get in return. The contract also would tell us what additional costs to expect if we had to move to assisted living or to the nursing home.

Retired couples often come to Asbury after selling their homes and using the proceeds to pay the entrance fee for a single-family villa or an apartment. The standard entrance fee for a villa ranges from $243,000 to $281,000. For an apartment, the entry fee ranges from $44,000 to $215,000. Residents of villas pay a monthly fee from $591 to $625. In the apartments, singles pay a monthly fee from $896 to $1889, depending on the size of the apartment. There is an extra $379 monthly charge for a couple.

In addition to the villas and apartments, there are other apartments—called Asbury Suites—for people who need assisted living.

There are no entry fees for persons who enter Asbury from the outside community and go directly into assisted living or for persons who move from independent living to assisted living. Monthly fees in assisted living are tied to the level of care required, of which there are six. The monthly fee in Asbury Suites for level-one care is $3278 for a single person; at level six, the monthly fee rises to $5369 for a single person. The rate for couples depends on the level of care required by each spouse. The entrance fee does not offer any equity ownership in a villa or apartment. However, it is possible to get a refund of one's entrance fee under the following circumstances:

Any incoming resident who is willing to pay the standard fee, plus 45 percent extra, can get a 90 percent refund when he or she dies or leaves the village. For the standard fee, plus 80 percent extra, the person can get a 100 percent refund. (No interest is paid on the refund.) Seventy percent of new residents pay the standard entry fee; 30 percent opt for the 90 percent or 100 percent refund.

Asbury is one of many CCRCs in the Washington area. Each one is different. Housing, recreation facilities, entrance fees, monthly charges, and contracts all vary. People in the CCRC business like to say, "When you've seen one CCRC, you've seen one CCRC."

If you're interested in a CCRC, the best advice is: Shop around. If you want to move into a CCRC, consult a lawyer before signing any contract.

CCRC contracts generally fall into three categories, all of which include housing and residential services, but differ in the amount of health care they cover and in how you pay for accommodations, services, and health care: Here are some definitions:

- The "extensive" or "A-type" contract provides for the pre-payment of health care expenses in a manner similar to an insurance arrangement; it is sometimes known as a "life care agreement." Extensive agreements offer the most health-related services for one predetermined monthly fee.

- The "modified" or "B-type" contract includes a specified amount of long-term health care in the monthly fee. Additional health care beyond the prepaid amount is available on a fee-for-service basis.
- The "fee-for-service" or "C-type" contract does not include long-term health care in its monthly fee. While residents receive priority admission to the nursing care facility, they pay the full daily rate.

Asbury is a C-type, or fee-for-service, institution. If Sara and I were residents of Asbury and had to go into the nursing facility, it would cost $161 a day, or $4830 a month, for a private room. However, our long-term-care policy would pay $110 a day. If and when we ran out of money, we probably would be eligible for the Maryland Medicaid program, which pays for nursing home costs. At present, 27 percent of Asbury's nursing home residents are on Medicaid. The Asbury Foundation also helps out: In 1999, it contributed $1.9 million to care for 222 residents.

"We have never put anybody out in the community because they couldn't afford to stay here," John Capasso told me. However, even a nonprofit institution such as Asbury has to be run like a business to stay in business, Capasso explained, and the income Asbury receives from monthly fees doesn't always cover its expenses. "The things that keep us a going concern," he said, "are the entrance fees and the ability to invest that money. The return on investment helps cover operating expenses."

It all makes sense, of course. But it also makes me wish we had saved more money during our working years. One of these days, we may need it.

The future of long-term-care insurance

The arrival of the twenty-first century was accompanied by a growing awareness in the nation's capital and elsewhere that the retirement of 77 million baby boomers, due to begin in 2010, is certain to have a huge impact on the demand for long-term medical care services and on the nation's health care costs. As noted earlier, in 2000 there were 35 million Americans who were 65 or older. By 2025, there will be 62 million Americans age 65 and above. And by 2050, there will be 80 million older Americans. If our present health care system remains intact, all these people will receive health care benefits from Medicare or Medicaid. The cost of their benefits could rise to levels that would prove to be unsustainable.

Medicare and Medicaid costs have been rising sharply for some years. And in 2001 they will still be going up—even before the first wave of baby boomers hits age 65. Medicare benefits in fiscal year 2000, which ended September 30, cost $219.8 billion. In fiscal 2001, the cost will be $240.2 billion, a one-year increase of 9.3 percent.

One "immediate" problem facing Congress is that, in 2023, as more and more baby boomers demand more and more medical services, the Medicare Hospital Insurance trust fund that pays hospital bills (Part A) is expected to run out of money. Congress has been debating ways to prevent this unthinkable event from occurring. Meanwhile, the Medicaid program, which will provide health care services to about 34 million low-income people in fiscal-year 2001 also faces rising costs, according to Nancy-Ann DeParle, HCFA administrator.

Federal Medicaid expenditures in fiscal 2001 are estimated to be more than $124 billion, an increase of about 7 percent, or $8 billion, over fiscal-year 2000. Combined federal and state expenditures for Medicaid were expected to reach $219 billion in 2001, of which the federal share was about 57 percent. So the problem is clear: too many people drawing more benefits than the government may be able to pay. A national bipartisan commission spent many months during 1999 looking for an answer to the problem, but in the end, the group could not put together enough votes to make a recommendation.

Here are some of the events taking place that will have a bearing on the American health problem:

Congress had hoped to save money on Medicare by steering millions of Medicare recipients to managed care organizations. Complying with a congressional mandate, HCFA created the six-option Medicare Plus Choice program. However, some 18 months after the plans were authorized, few insurance or health care companies have come forward to offer the programs to the public. Among the reasons they haven't are that the health care companies felt that the administrative burdens and fees imposed by HCFA were too high and the reimbursements too low.

Congress and the White House began to recognize the plight of America's caregivers and the ailing individuals that they care for. *Health Affairs* magazine has reported that 15.8 million Americans spend an average of 18 hours a week caring for ailing relatives. Their services were estimated to be worth $196 billion a year.

In his 2000 State of the Union message, President Clinton proposed giving a $3000 annual tax credit to individuals with long-term-care needs or to their caregivers to help cover long-term-care expenses. The plan won support from a bipartisan coalition in Congress, but its passage remained uncertain in the spring of 2000. The cost was estimated at $8.8 billion over 5 years and $26.6 billion over 10 years.

Long-term-care insurance began to take center stage in Washington, D.C. At the end of 1999, an estimated 6.5 million long-term-care policies had been sold in this country, according to the Health Insurance Association of America. About 500,000 new policies are sold each year, with about 80 percent bought by individuals or through fraternal or service associations.

At last count, about 120 insurance companies were selling long-term-care policies. The business seems destined to grow as baby boomers become aware of the financial drubbing they could take if they have to "spend down" their savings to qualify for a Medicaid-financed stay in a nursing home.

In 1996, the long-term-care business got a boost from the passage of the Health Insurance Portability and Accountability Act. The act made premiums partially tax deductible if you itemize your deductions and if your health care spending reaches 7.5 percent of adjusted gross income. However, only about 4.5 percent of all tax returns report medical expenses as itemized deductions. So it does not appear that many taxpayers are benefiting by that feature of the 1996 law.

In the spring of 2000, a major congressional and lobbying effort got under way to make long-term-care insurance more attractive by granting a "100 percent income tax deduction" for the cost of buying a policy. I've put the words "100 percent income tax deduction" in quotes because it's clear that, even if the bill is adopted, it would be difficult for taxpayers actually to get a full 100 percent deduction for the cost of their long-term-care insurance premiums.

The bill was introduced by Democrats and Republicans from the Senate and the House. The sponsors were Senators Charles Grassley (R-Iowa) and Bob Graham (D-Florida) and Representatives Nancy Johnson (R-Connecticut) and Karen Thurman (D-Florida). The bill also had the support of AARP and HIAA.

The plan would phase in the aforementioned deduction, but limit the amount that could be deducted according to the age of the policyholder. Thus, an individual under age 55 could deduct 60 percent of the cost of the policy in the first year, plus an additional 10 percent a year until the percentage would reach 100 percent in the fourth year. For an individual over age 55, the deduction would begin at 70 percent in the first year, go to 85 percent the second, and then to 100 percent in the third year. However, deductions would be limited by age restrictions already in the tax codes. As of 2000, they were as follows: a $220 limit for those who are age 40 or less; $410 for those age 41 to 50; $820 for age 51 to 60; $2200 for age 61 to 70; and $2750 over age 70.

The bill's sponsors estimated the cost in lost tax revenues as $741 million over 5 years and $7.3 billion over 10 years. The bill is far less grandiose than the legislation envisioned by an earlier HIAA study which estimated that the cost of the lost taxes would be $3.1 billion to $3.5 billion over 5 years. The study also said that the cost would be offset by future reductions in Medicaid spending at the state and federal levels. The study concluded that the long-term-care tax deduction would make such policies more affordable and, as a result, would lead to a 14 to 24 percent increase in the numbers of people willing to buy long-term care-insurance.

Whether or not the proposed tax deduction is adopted, the importance of long-term-care insurance is certain to get a big boost from the decision to allow federal employees, their families, and members of the military to buy long-term-care insurance as part of their government health care coverage. Employees would pay the full cost of coverage.

There are now 9.3 million people in the Federal Employee Health Benefits program, including 1.8 million active employees. When members of the armed services are added, the total eligible pool for long-term-care coverage would number 13 million. Congressional approval of the plan has put the government's stamp of approval on the concept of long-term-care insurance. That endorsement, together with the number of new policies sold, would constitute a huge boost for the long-term-care insurance industry. And because the company or companies that are selected to provide policies for government workers would be under tight control by the government, adoption of the bill could lead to important refinements in the quality and cost of policies sold outside the government. And that would be a great step forward!

For more information

The following are several organizations that can provide information on home care, assisted-living facilities, small group homes, nursing homes, and continuing-care retirement communities:

- The American Association of Homes and Services for the Aging. (AAHSA) publishes *The Consumers' Directory of Continuing Care Retirement Communities*, which profiles more than 500 CCRCs and includes information on services, agreement options, and costs. The book can be ordered by calling 800-508-9442 or faxing orders to 770-442-9742. The cost is $25 for AAHSA members, $35 for nonmembers. The organization's Web site is www.aahsa.org.
- The Assisted Living Federation of America (703-691-8100) offers a free package of consumer information, including an "Assisted Living Guide and Check List." The group's Web site is www.alfa.org.
- The National Association for Home Care of Washington, DC, offers an on-line guide to choosing a home care provider, as well as other consumer information. The Web site is www.nahc.org.
- The American Health Care Association represents long-term-care and assisted-living providers. For free information on long-term health care options, call 202-842-4444. The group's Web site is www.acha.org.
- The Consumer Consortium on Assisted Living (CCAL) publishes a booklet titled *Choosing an Assisted Living Facility: Strategies for Making the Right Decision*. The publication is available on CCAL's Web site, www.ccal.org, or by mail. Send $5 to CCAL, P. O. Box 3375, Arlington, VA, 22203. Or order by phone at 703-533-8121.
- The National Association of Professional Geriatric Care Managers helps families coordinate care for parents or spouses who need medical treatment or assistance with daily tasks. Fees vary. The association publishes *The GCM Consumer Directory*, available for $15. For information, call 520-881-8008.

A number of organizations provide information on long-term-care insurance and suggestions on how to shop for policies:

- For more information about long-term-care insurance, get a copy of *Long-Term Care Planning: A Dollar and Sense Guide*, published by United Seniors Health Cooperative (USHC), Washington, D.C. This easy-to-read 100-page book is available for $18.95, including shipping, from USHC, 409 Third St. SW, Washington, DC 20024.
- The State Health Insurance Assistance Program has counselors in many communities across the country who can offer advice on Medicare, Medicaid, medigap, and long-term-care insurance. Phone numbers of local counselors are listed in the back of the booklet *Medicare and You 2000*, which is sent to most Medicare recipients. The information also is available at www.medicare.gov .
- Weiss Ratings, Inc., 4176 Burns Rd., Palm Beach Gardens, FL 33410 publishes financial safety ratings for life and health insurers, HMOs, and Blue Cross/Blue Shield and related plans, among others. Ratings are available on the telephone at $15 per company. Call 1-800-289-9222. *A Consumer Guide to Long-Term Care Insurance*, customized for your age, gender, and address, is available for $49. A *Health Insurance Report for Seniors* provides a customized report on the cost of medigap policies. The publication is available for $49. Weiss Ratings' Web site is www.weissratings.com.

DECISION 10

Where do I want to live after I retire?

The question of where to live after you retire can have a certain "Fantasy Island" quality. It's easy to imagine yourself retiring and moving to that fabulous vacation spot where you spent two weeks soaking up the sun and scuba diving. Wouldn't it be great fun to live there full time?

Or perhaps you can see yourself moving to that great little town in the West where you went to college. If you lived there, you could wake up in the morning and look at the mountains where you love to hike. And you could take some of those history courses you didn't have time for when you were in school. What a pleasant life that would be!

Over the years, Sara and I have watched many of our friends and relatives pursue their retirement dreams by packing up and moving to places where they found a better climate, a more interesting lifestyle, or a lower cost of living. Often, I've noticed, retirement moves are determined by the whereabouts of family members. Many of the people who live in our retirement community came here from distant places because they have children and grandchildren who live nearby. They moved to be closer to them.

Surely, one of the lessons of growing older is that it's highly desirable, when you are in your retirement years, to be close to family. Because illness is always a possibility, you never know when you might need help. It might be help with simple things, like getting to a doctor's appointment or going to the supermarket. Or, on a more serious note, it might be the help and comfort of having family members nearby when you go into the hospital for surgery.

Being close to family has many dimensions, of course. For many retirees, including me, the opportunity to spend time with children, and especially with grandchildren, can be the best part of retirement. I like to think it is rewarding for the grandchildren as well. Even so, a discussion of retirees who move—or who don't move—always comes down to this old idea: "Different strokes for different folks." The decision to move or to stay is very much an individual matter, and each retiree has to make his or her own judgment on where to go—or whether to go at all.

Our Florida investigation

A year after I retired, Sara and I thought seriously about leaving the Washington, D.C., area and moving to Florida. There were at least a couple of good reasons to make the move: We would get away from the ice and snow of Washington winters. And we would be closer to many of our relatives and friends who live in the Sunshine State, including Sara's four sisters.

But there were also several good reasons to stay: We had lived in the Washington area for more than 25 years. Our children and grandchildren were all nearby. So were the doctors and dentists we'd used for many years. We also felt very much at home. We had become attached to the city's great monuments and cultural attractions. And we liked the small communities of suburban Maryland and Virginia.

The idea of moving also raised several hard questions. First, were we ready to put forth the physical and psychological effort that moving requires? Only a few years earlier, we had sold our big five-bedroom house and moved to a small two-bedroom apartment in our retirement community. The memory of that move was fresh in our minds, and I, for one, wasn't sure I was ready for another move.

Second, what would it cost us to move to south Florida? Where would we live? How much would we have to spend for housing? And how would the cost of living in Florida compare with the cost of living in the Washington area?

These are the kinds of questions that face all retirees who are thinking of moving, whether they're considering the Sunbelt areas of the country, such as Florida and Arizona, or the newly popular retirement communities of the West and Pacific Northwest. One thing is sure: No matter where you want to go to retire, choosing a place to live requires a considerable amount of research. And frankly, the process is pretty much the same whether you are heading north, south, east, or west.

Sara and I did some in-depth research when we were thinking of moving to south Florida. The process would have been the same if we had been going to any other area of the country. You could easily repeat this type of research for any destination that interests you. In any event, this is what we did:

We took a trip to south Florida and spent three weeks in Broward County and Palm Beach County, where we made a fairly intensive effort to get to know the local communities. Although the weather in the region can be unpredictable at times, we were there during a period of warmth and sunshine.

Clearly, Florida's biggest drawing card is a pleasant climate during the winter months. In mid-February, I swam and played golf under blue skies and bright sunshine, with temperatures in the eighties. I wore short-sleeved shirts and shorts on days that my friends at home were dressed in parkas and using their snow shovels to dig out from under a big storm.

In the course of our visit, Sara and I tried to get a sense of what it would be like to live in Florida full time. I was particularly interested in whether it would be cheaper to live in Florida than in the high-priced Washington area. Cost was important to us, as it probably will be to you, because, like many retirees, Sara and I are trying to make our retirement dollars last as long as possible.

Cheaper housing, smaller tax bills

To get a line on the cost of housing in south Florida, we visited several new housing developments. We studied and compared prices and the quality of the housing being offered. We also tried to find out as much as we could about the local communities and the facilities and services that were available to residents.

We talked with friends and relatives about their housing experiences. Sara and I visited our cousins, Marvin and Barbara Cohn, who recently bought a new one-floor, four-bedroom, two-and-a-half-bath home on a giant artificial lake in Pembroke Pines, a rapidly growing community in south Broward County. Marvin, a broker who deals in commercial and industrial real estate, told me that his basic house cost $167,000. The lakefront site cost another $33,000, and he installed a $30,000 swimming pool. Then the Cohns upgraded various aspects of the house, including the tile floors, kitchen appliances, cabinets, and lighting. The upgrades cost about $30,000. That made the total cost of this bright and airy high-ceilinged house about $260,000, not counting furnishings. Although I am no real estate expert, I think it would be fair to report that the Cohns' house, if located in the Washington, D.C., area, would cost $500,000 to $600,000.

I also talked to my former Maryland neighbor, Walter Packer, who moved to Boynton Beach, Florida, in 1999. His new apartment cost $130,000, he said. But he was quite sure that a similar apartment in his old Silver Spring, Maryland, neighborhood would cost at least $200,000. It soon became obvious to me that housing in south Florida is much less expensive.

I asked Packer about the cost of food in Florida. Packer, who spent 25 years in the grocery business, has a keen eye for food prices and quality. In Florida, Packer said, he finds that fruits and vegetables are 20 percent cheaper, and groceries generally are 10 percent to 15 percent cheaper than in Maryland. Restaurant meals in Florida also tend to be less costly, Packer said, especially during "early bird" seating hours, which usually start around 5 or 5:30 P.M. These reduced-price meals are so popular that the "early bird" has been jokingly dubbed the state bird of Florida.

I was able to informally confirm Packer's view that food prices are lower in Florida by pricing a "basket" of 16 items in a popular supermarket in the Boca Raton area and in a popular supermarket in Rockville, Maryland. The items cost $40.74 in Florida, $52.30 in Maryland.

When I looked at the price of clothing in Florida, it seemed to be about the same as in Maryland. But we wouldn't need winter wardrobes, although we would need additional summer clothes. Then there was the matter of how much it would cost us to relocate. I was sure that it would cost several thousands of dollars, but at that point I had not yet tried to come up with a firm figure.

When I got home from south Florida, I continued my research by phone and found that if we moved, we would save quite a bit of money on taxes. That was chiefly because Florida, unlike Maryland, Virginia, and the District of Columbia, has no state income taxes. That could mean a significant saving for us, since we are residents of Maryland. I knew how much I paid each year in Maryland taxes. But as a journalist, I was curious how much retired couples living in the D.C. area paid in state taxes.

I asked certified public accountant and tax expert William A. Fritz, Jr., of Fritz & Co. in Fairfax City, Virginia, to help me figure it out. We made these assumptions: The couples were over 65 and had annual incomes before taxes of $77,000, with $30,000 coming from Social Security, $42,000 from pensions, and $5000 from interest on investments.

If the couples take the standard deductions, Bill Fritz said, they would pay state income taxes of $2610 in Maryland, $2282 in the District, and $480 in Virginia. By moving to Florida, the couples would save those amounts. (The Virginia tax is considerably lower, Fritz told me, because the state grants a $12,000 "age deduction" for individuals over 65. Thus, a Virginia couple would get a $24,000 deduction.)

However, there was another aspect to the Florida tax situation that is important to anyone thinking of moving to the state: Florida levies what it calls an "intangible tax" on an individual's total investments, including stocks, bonds, mutual funds, and money market funds. The state does not count bank deposits, certificates of deposit, annuities, U.S. government obligations, Florida state or municipal bonds, or retirement accounts such as 401(k) or Keogh plans.

I asked Martin R. Glickstein, a certified public accountant in Winter Park, Florida, for an explanation, and he said that this is how the tax works: Individual taxpayers with assets under $100,000 pay $1 per thousand and get a $20 deduction. Individuals with assets over $100,000 pay $1.50 per thousand and get a $70 deduction. Married taxpayers with assets under $200,000 pay $1 per thousand and get a $40 deduction. Married taxpayers with assets over $200,000 pay $1.50 per thousand and get a $140 deduction.

Florida also offers discounts of as much as 4 percent for early filing. Thus, a couple with $150,000 of taxable assets would pay just $105.60 on the intangible tax if they filed early. If the tax that is due before the discount is less than $60, the taxpayer is not required to pay any tax, although the state wants the taxpayer to file a tax form anyway, Glickstein said.

As regards sales taxes, Maryland has a 5 percent tax, Virginia's tax is 4.5 percent, and the District's tax is 5.75 percent. The Florida tax is 6 percent. However, some counties in Florida add surcharges, making the sales tax 6.5 percent, 7 percent, or even 7.5 percent in a few counties. Meanwhile, legal residents of Florida are entitled to a so-called homestead exemption on their personal residences. This feature reduces the assessed valuation of a house by $25,000, which, in turn, reduces the homeowner's tax bill.

Dealing with the summer heat

Three weeks in south Florida and my follow-up research gave me lots of information about what it would cost to live there. But the visit was valuable for another reason: It gave me a chance to talk to old friends about the year-round climate.

While full-time Florida residents like to boast of their sunny days in February, they are less enthusiastic about the heat, humidity, and rain that can stifle outdoor activity in July and August. Our friends Milton and Shirley Schrenzel of Del Ray Beach have lived in Florida full time for the past 10 years. However, in the summer, we are likely to find them in Vermont or somewhere in the Northeast, visiting one of their five grown children.

A retired schoolteacher, Shirley Schrenzel described south Florida's summer rainy season as "endless days" of heat and humidity. "You have the phenomenon of living a totally air-conditioned existence," she said. "For some people, that's no problem. In our case, there's a need for a change of pace, a change of weather, and a change from Florida." Milton Schrenzel, a retired manufacturer, said he thought their schedule brought them "the best of both worlds."

The Schrenzels noted that many people do not leave Florida in summer because they are unable or unwilling to go very far from their doctors or hospitals. "The older one gets, the more scary it becomes to have to deal with a brand new medical team," Shirley Schrenzel said.

Moving and adjusting

As Sara and I mulled over the idea of moving to Florida, we talked about the process of adjusting to a new state and a new community. We realized that if we moved, we'd have to adjust not only to a new climate, but to a new home, new geography, new cities and towns, new highways, new newspapers and TV stations, new libraries, new businesses, and new customs. For instance, while I was visiting Florida, I couldn't find a bank that was open on Saturdays, and that was rather annoying.

Of course, before we moved, we would have to sell our apartment in Maryland and buy a new home or apartment in Florida and then furnish it. That would be a guaranteed hassle that would discourage me, but probably not Sara. She is a very good organizer and handled our last move quite efficiently.

As I mentioned, it has been only a few years since we sold the house we lived in for 25 years and moved five miles away to our present condominium apartment in a high-rise building. But I can easily remember the feeling of loss when we left the old neighbor-hood, with its familiar faces and shopkeepers who called you by your first name. And I can also remember the strangeness of get-ting used to a new home in new surroundings, even though we hadn't moved a great distance.

One possible alternative to a full-fledged move was to become a "snowbird"—someone who goes south in the winter and north in the summer. That is what some of our friends and relatives did. They bought small and relatively inexpensive apartments in Florida, often fully furnished, which they use for three or four months during the winter. But they keep their homes in the Northeast and thus do not have to deal with Florida weather in the summer.

That would mean finding the money for a second home. If we could do so, the arrangement would have many advantages. We'd be close to our children and grandchildren in the north most of the year; indeed, they'd probably insist on coming to Florida to visit us during winter holidays! We'd be close to our Florida rela-tives for several months—long enough to enjoy their company, but not long enough to wear out our welcome.

Sara, however, was dubious about having two homes to worry about. Not only would it be a financial strain, she said, but she feared that problems could arise in either home when we were away at the other. So we slowly dropped the idea of having two homes.

That left one option: a full-time move to Florida. Several neighbors had recently done that, and they reported that things had worked out well for them. While we were weighing the pros and cons of making the big move, several other factors began to dominate our thinking and eventually persuaded us to stay in the Washington area. Those factors involved our children and, espe-cially, our grandchildren.

When I discussed relocating in one of my *Washington Post* columns, I received a dozen letters from readers offering their opinions. One of the most persuasive letters came from a woman who told us about her mother's move to Florida. Although her mother came north to visit occasionally, the daughter said, her mother missed seeing her grandchildren grow up and in many ways lost touch with her daughter's family.

The message in the letter was clear: Don't do it. The more we talked about moving, the more we came back to the question of whether a move would cause us to lose touch with our young grandchildren. We kept thinking of that old saying, "Out of sight, out of mind."

But there was one other important factor: If the time came when one of us became seriously ill, we did not want to be living in Florida, far from our children. That would force our kids to fly to Florida to deal with our health problems.

Sara and I had been through that experience with my parents, who were occasional snowbirds. When my father became ill, Sara and I went to Florida to bring them back to our home. When Sara's brother became seriously ill, his son spent many weeks commuting between New York and Florida. We had seen many other examples of that kind of event.

Finally, when we weighed all our reasons for moving against all our reasons for staying, we decided to stay.

Making the move in stages

If you are going to relocate, one of the best ways to do it is over a period of years. My former neighbor, Walter Packer, the friend who helped me compare Florida and Maryland housing and grocery prices, was a snowbird for many years. He and his wife, Roni Packer, owned two homes, one in Silver Spring, Maryland, and one in West Palm Beach, Florida. They lived in the Washington area for 40 years.

In 1999, the couple decided it was time to make a permanent move to Florida. They sold their apartment in Silver Spring, rented their home in West Palm Beach, and bought a new apartment in

Boynton Beach. Essentially, the Packers made their move in stages. Each year, they stayed in Florida for longer and longer periods to make sure they really wanted to move some day. "That was done by design," Packer said, acknowledging that he never cared much for the sun, the ocean, or the heat. But, over the years, with the help of air-conditioning, Packer said, he has gotten used to the climate of south Florida.

One of the things that kept the Packers from moving even sooner was the fact that they have two married daughters, a married son, and five grandchildren living in the Washington, D.C., area. They were reluctant to leave the area, especially when their grandchildren were young. But as time went on, their grandchildren grew up and became busier and busier with school and other activities, Packer told me. "It became somewhat of a hit-and-miss proposition as to when we could get to see them and be with them," Packer said.

Finally, the Packers decided that they could move and still maintain close contact with their children and grandchildren by coming north three or four times a year to celebrate holidays and special family events such as graduations. On those occasions, they would be able to see all the members of their family. They also could remain in touch by telephone.

There were two other reasons that helped persuade the couple to move, Packer said. One was that Florida does not have a state income tax. "We found it a great saving being here in Florida and not having the Maryland state tax to contend with," Packer said. The other element was the Packers' desire to get away from the expense of maintaining two homes.

Packer said he and his wife are happy they made the move. "We're very comfortable. We've made new friends. We renewed acquaintances with some old friends. We've met members of my family who live here permanently, and we've really settled in to a comfortable lifestyle," Packer added. "We've gotten quite active in our clubhouse. Roni plays bridge and canasta. I play pinochle and cribbage. It's a very wonderful every-day-is-Sunday lifestyle."

Choosing a place to live

When Sara and I thought about moving, we considered going to Florida because of its climate and cost-of-living advantages. It was also where many of our friends and relatives lived. We felt that if you are going to make a major move at a late stage of life, it is reassuring to be close to family and friends.

But wherever you may want to go to retire, you are likely to face the same kinds of questions and dilemmas that we faced. Also, choosing a retirement community is no easy task. Ask David Savageau. For the past 20 years, this Boston native has been studying and writing about the best retirement communities in America. He is the author of *Retirement Places Rated* (New York: Macmillan Travel, 1999), a 324-page book that profiles 187 retirement areas across the United States and rates them for living costs, climate, services, crime, work opportunities, and recreation.

When I came across Savageau's book, I was awed by the extraordinary amount of research that went into its creation. As a reporter who has spent his life gathering information, I could appreciate the effort involved. So I was anxious to meet Savageau and get his thoughts about why retirees do or do not move and why some moves are successful and others are not.

Savageau has traveled extensively in the United States and has visited 150 of the 187 areas he has written about. In the course of his travels, he has had an opportunity to talk to many retirees about their relocation experiences, both good and bad. Savageau says people who are thinking about relocating should begin to plan their move long before they retire. "The decision to relocate should require at least five years in advance of the official day of retirement," he observed.

There is a well-established process that many people use to prepare for a retirement move, according to Savageau. Commonly, they spend vacations, both short and long, in an area they find attractive. In time, they may acquire a second home in the area, spending move and more time there in order to see whether they would be comfortable living there full time.

People need time, Savageau points out, to develop "a sense of place." Some people, he notes, make the mistake of simply moving to Florida or Arizona without doing any research. When they find they don't like the climate or other aspects of those areas, they move again and again until they wind up back where they started, saying, "There's no place like home."

Despite all the talk about moving, Savageau said, U.S. Census Bureau figures show that less than 5 percent of people over 60 move between states. When he first began studying mobility patterns in the 1980s, he says, climate was the main reason that retirees moved. And almost all the movement was to the Sunbelt states. While climate is still a factor today, he notes, the cost of living is currently the major reason for relocation. The desire to save money prompts many retirees to go to less expensive communities where housing is cheaper and taxes are lower.

Retirees also are expanding their destinations, with the Pacific Northwest becoming a popular relocation choice. Savageau has counted 40 states that are now seeing newcomers. Indeed, he says, before you move to any retirement community, find out whether you are likely to be welcomed by local residents. If the community is not hospitable to newcomers, you may not want to move there.

Places that are used to seeing and welcoming newcomers include college towns, areas near military bases, and vacation and resort areas. It is in those places, Savageau suggests, that retirees are likely to find it relatively easy to make new friends. Making new friends and developing a satisfying social life are vital to any successful relocation, he says.

Trying to find friends fast

I know what Savageau is talking about. Although Sara and I did not move to Florida, we did move locally to a brand new 300-family apartment complex in a retirement community. We found ourselves among a diverse group of people who had one main thing in common: They were all new residents. And they all wanted to make friends fast.

This was our third such experience. On two previous occasions we moved to new single-family housing developments where, each time, everybody in the neighborhood was new, and they, too, all wanted to make friends fast. What happens in these circumstances is a lot like the Great Land Rush. Your phone begins to ring with calls from your new neighbors, and your mailbox is soon stuffed with invitations for cocktails, brunch, and dinner. Then the games begin. It may be poker, bridge, canasta, or mah-jong. After that, you begin to get invitations to join a club: the Lions or the Kiwanis or Rotary or Knights of Columbus or American Legion, etc.

Then you hear from the fun bunch. "We're going to the water-walking class on Wednesdays. Would you like to join us?" Or "We need a few more singers in our little theater group. We're doing the *Mikado*. Won't you come down and try out?" That's how it all begins. You can probably guess how most of these overtures will end.

At the cocktail party, your new neighbors all seemed like they'd rather be someplace else, except for the guy in the corner. You spent most of the evening listening to him talk about his gall-bladder surgery. His story took longer than the operation.

At the dinner party, the food was good. But the other three couples all seemed to know each other from their old neighborhood. So they spent most of the evening talking about people and places they all knew. None of it meant anything to you.

At the brunch, you met an interesting couple, and it seemed like you could be friends. The only problem was that they spend most of their time on cruises. In fact, they were heading out the next morning on their forty-third cruise. It didn't seem like they'd have much time to spend with you.

You joined the poker game and played for about six weeks, but you quit because one of the players complained constantly about his bad luck. So you made an excuse about working late and left. The canasta game also broke up about a month after it began, because two of the players said the other two players were too slow.

Friends were easier to find at the service clubs and at the fraternal organizations. And although you didn't get a singing role in the *Mikado*, it was fun helping with the costumes, and you became friendly with several people who, coincidentally, had joined the water-walking class. So you joined, too.

In any event, a couple of years after we moved to each of our new communities, we had a whole new set of friends. Of course, they didn't include any of the people we first met when we arrived. We found friends in our own way and at our own pace.

That outcome is very much in keeping with research findings gathered by Cathy Goodwin, professor of marketing at Nova Southeastern University in Fort Lauderdale, Florida. Goodwin is the author of *Making the Big Move* (Oakland, CA: New Harbinger Publications, 1999). She has lived all over North America, from Connecticut to California and from Alaska to Florida. Having moved frequently, she has developed a keen sense of what it takes to adjust to life in a new community.

Goodwin is a strong believer in the take-it-slow approach. All too often, she says, new arrivals rush to get involved in community activities and make new friends. "There's a real tendency to charge in and say 'I want to feel at home right away.'" But that's not the way to go, she adds. "It takes two years at a minimum to feel at home in a new place."

Goodwin suggests that people wait a while before trying to make new friends or getting involved with volunteer activities. She reasons as follows: The people you initially become friendly with after you move in are unlikely to still be your friends by the time your second year rolls around. By then, you probably will have found friends you like better. But by then, it may be difficult to get away from some of your earlier acquaintances.

The same rule applies when it comes to volunteering for community activities, Goodwin says. It's a good idea to wait until you become familiar with the volunteer opportunities that are available. Some volunteer jobs will be far more interesting than others. "When you're new, you don't know what the good stuff is." And if you don't wait long enough to find out, she adds, you could lock yourself into activities that might be hard to get out of.

Of course, if you don't move, you won't have to worry about finding new friends. But many retirees do move, and for good reasons. And the evidence is that they find communities and friends they enjoy and are happy that they made the move. It can be done. Just look before you leap.

For more information

Goodwin, Cathy. *Making the Big Move."* New Harbinger Publications, Inc., Oakland, CA, 1999.

Howells, John. *Where to Retire: America's Best and Most Affordable Places."* Gateway, Oakland, CA, 1998.

Savageau, David. *Retirement Places Rated.* Macmillan Travel, New York, NY, 1999.

How should I arrange my estate to save on taxes and avoid probate?

Living in a retirement village has many advantages: no grass to mow, no leaves to rake, and no snow to shovel. It also has some drawbacks, one of which is that we live among a large group of elderly people. Thus, it is not unusual to hear that one of our neighbors has died. While we are sad to hear such news, we are not surprised. The people who live in this community are in their sixties, seventies, and eighties. Some are even in their nineties. And while most of the people we know lead active, busy lives, we are aware that sooner or later the aging process takes its toll.

For Sara and me, the deaths of neighbors are reminders of our own physical vulnerabilities. Although we're both feeling well, the memory of our medical experiences has focused our attention on whether we are properly prepared for the day—hopefully, far off—when one or both of us will die.

In this complicated world, we have discovered that death is not only an emotional event; it is also a legal event and even a taxable one. A favorable outcome depends on advance planning, getting good advice, and carefully assembling your financial records and documents.

The decision to organize our financial and family affairs did not come easily. Like most people, we weren't eager to think about dying. And there was even less incentive to think about wills and trusts and estate taxes, subjects that ordinarily would make our eyes glaze over. But Sara and I talked it over and decided that whether we liked it or not, one of these days we would have to depart. And that being the case, we wanted to do what we could to achieve three goals: One, we wanted to depart in a neat and orderly way, creating the least amount of stress for our children. Two, we wanted to make sure that our heirs would get what we wanted them to get. And, three, we wanted our estate to be settled with the smallest possible tax bill and the least amount of hassle.

To do all that, we got some good advice and made a series of decisions that will, we believe, accomplish those goals. Our guide through this legal jungle was Rhonda J. Macdonald, an attorney and certified public accountant, whose office is in Vienna, Virginia. Macdonald is a specialist in wills, trusts and, other estate-planning matters.

I think it is fair to say that the process we went through in making our estate-planning decisions was a learning experience. Sara and I both learned many things we never knew about what the law requires and about the opportunities that the law offers. And as a journalist writing about retirement-related matters, I learned things from other experts in estate planning that were both useful and surprising. In the course of this chapter, I will try to convey an understanding of what Sara and I did and what we learned.

It goes without saying that the experience of making an estate plan did not make me, in any sense, an expert on the subject. The story of what we did is merely that, and no more. It is certainly not a complete guide to estate planning. In fact, many aspects of estate planning are not even mentioned here, because we did not deal with them. Thus, if and when you focus on this aspect of retirement, you might have a very different experience from the one we had.

Planning ahead

The first thing that Sara and I did, even before we talked with Macdonald, was to arrange our funerals. We have a family burial plot, so we know where we're going to be laid to rest. And by making the arrangements with a funeral home in advance, we were able to negotiate the price and lock it in. This means that there'll be no additional charges, even if our funerals take place years from now. Also, we'll be able to pay for the cost over the next several years. All this means that our children won't have to rush around and make funeral arrangements in a crisis atmosphere. I've seen that happen to other people, and it's an unhappy sight.

But planning for your funeral is not—pardon the pun—the end of the story. Unfortunately, you also have to get ready for what happens before you die. Often, that involves a period of illness that may require its own kind of preparation.

When Sara and I met with Macdonald for the first time, we talked about what would happen if either of us became seriously ill to the point where we could no longer make our own decisions about our medical treatment. Macdonald recommended that we sign a document called an advance medical directive. In my case, it allows me to name Sara as the single individual who can make all my health care decisions for me if I am physically or mentally unable to do so. It also allows me to name an alternate person if she is not available.

Medical directives, Macdonald said, vary by state. Some states have a medical power of attorney and others a living will. In Virginia, where Macdonald is based, both types of medical directives have been combined into a single document called an "advance medical directive." The main purpose of my own advance medical directive is to make it clear that I do not want my doctors to keep me on life-support equipment or procedures if they decide that I have a terminal condition or that I am in a "persistent coma" from which there is no reasonable possibility of recovery. In those cases, I want them to understand that I would prefer to die naturally. Since I would be unable to tell that to my doctors directly, I also make it clear that I am relying on the document itself to be "the final expression of my legal right to refuse medical or surgical treatment."

While the wording of my document fully expresses my wishes and my hope that the doctors will follow my wishes, it isn't quite that simple. Macdonald explained that in virtually every hospital there is an ethics or other committee that will make the final decision on whether to "pull the plug" on a patient for whom there is no hope of recovery. That may take some time if the patient shows even the smallest life sign.

In my advance medical directive, it says that before any life-ending action can be taken, a medical team must decide whether I am able to make my own health care decisions. This decision is to be made by my physician, along with a second physician or clinical psychologist. After they examine me, they must submit a report in writing. Until they do, they can't withhold or withdraw treatment.

What role does my wife play in all this? As mentioned, in my directive I have given her the power to make all my health care decisions for me if I am unable to do so. These can be trivial decisions about my reactions to medication or far-reaching decisions about terminating my life. She is, in fact, authorized to make almost any medical decision for me, and she even has the power to direct the writing of a "no code" or "do not resuscitate" order. (Incidentally, when Sara signed her advance medical directive, she named me as her representative and gave me similar powers.)

Because Macdonald has her office in Virginia, the advance medical directive that we signed is a Virginia version. Macdonald noted that these directives vary from state to state, but added, "My experience, happily, has been that a living will validly executed in any state is honored in another state."

A matter of trust

On more than one occasion over the years, Sara and I have watched friends and relatives try to deal with one of life's most difficult problems: the mental incapacitation of a spouse or parent because of a stroke or the swift onset of Alzheimer's disease. When that happens, especially because of a stroke, the stricken individual may suddenly lose his or her ability to make informed legal and financial decisions. What is needed, therefore, is a way to appoint a spouse or child to make those decisions for the person who is ill. That way, Macdonald told us, is to sign a general durable power of attorney, a document that allows Sara and me to appoint each other to act for each other in the event that either one of us can no longer make our own financial and legal decisions. In a way, the durable power of attorney resembles our advance medical directives—except that the durable power of attorney deals with financial matters rather than health matters.

The powers granted in a durable power of attorney are extremely broad. In essence, Sara and I have given each other almost complete power over the financial side of our lives. For instance, my power of attorney allows my wife to gain access to my bank accounts, to manage or even sell my real estate, to sell or transfer my investments, and more. And, of course, Sara has given me the same powers.

While these powers are sweeping, Macdonald said, they often are needed in a hurry when a spouse becomes mentally incapacitated. Even so, she said, the original document should be kept in a safe place from which it will not be removed until the person who signed it becomes incapacitated. Macdonald cautioned us that such documents become effective immediately when you sign them, not just when you become ill. She said she tells clients that they should have a high level of trust in the person to whom they give their power of attorney. In other words, make sure you really trust each other.

Those sweetheart wills

At this point, Sara and I were feeling somewhat self-satisfied with our progress. We'd been able to make advance funeral plans, and we managed to understand and sign two complicated legal documents: medical directives and powers of attorney. But, as we soon discovered, that was only the beginning of our learning experience in estate planning. We had a long way to go.

Essentially, we were taking a quick course in wills, trusts, and estate taxes. Macdonald was a patient instructor, always willing to explain an obscure concept over and over again until we understood. And there was much to understand. Estate planning is an extremely complicated field, especially for a person who is not a lawyer and can't even do his own tax return. But thanks to Macdonald, I finally began to understand that estate planning has many advantages.

Macdonald says that married people who come to see her often bring her what she calls sweetheart wills. That's the kind of will in which the husband leaves everything to his wife and the wife leaves everything to her husband. Indeed, that's the kind of wills that Sara and I had before we began to work with Macdonald.

Here's how sweetheart wills work: If I die, I can leave everything I own to Sara, tax free. The problem arises when she dies. At that point, the total dollar value of her estate, minus a one-person exemption of $1 million (for deaths occurring in 2002 or 2003) will be subject to estate tax. Thus, while "sweetheart" wills are romantic, they won't keep Uncle Sam from taking a big bite out of your estate after the second spouse dies. Nor will it avoid the expense and delays of going through probate court.

What is probate? Generally speaking, it's a legal process that is used to wind up a deceased person's financial affairs. The personal representative or executor who is named in the will prepares an inventory of the assets and liabilities of the estate, pays any taxes and bills that are due, and makes sure that the heirs get the bequests that have been left to them. But all of those items have to be approved or at least reviewed by the court. Many people try to avoid probate court, because of the time it takes to settle an estate and the filing fees involved.

Macdonald told us that the best way to avoid or minimize both federal estate taxes and probate is to create a "revocable living trust" for each spouse, which is used to hold the assets belonging to each. The trust also constitutes what is called a "bypass trust," meaning that when each partner dies, the assets in the trust will escape federal taxes up to a certain dollar limit.

Now, even after we decided to create two living trusts, Sara and I still needed wills. In our wills, we each named a personal representative and specified their duties. Our wills described how we want our personal property to be distributed and gave other instructions on winding up our financial affairs. However, detailed instructions about who inherits what and when and how are all stated in our trust documents.

By creating two bypass trusts, we were setting the stage so we could take advantage of an important federal tax exemption. It provides that, during their lifetimes, a couple can each transfer a certain amount of money to children or other beneficiaries, without incurring gift or estate taxes. That exemption, as shown in Table 11-1, is continuing to rise through 2009.

This is the way the system works:

If the husband dies first, the bypass trust shelters his estate tax exemption from estate taxes and from probate. When his wife dies, the trust shelters her estate tax exemption from estate taxes and probate. That allows a total of $2 million in assets (for deaths occurring in 2002 and 2003) to be distributed to the couple's beneficiaries without federal estate taxes. Depending on where the couple lives, however, state taxes may be due.

By comparison, Macdonald said, having only sweetheart wills can be very expensive for a couple with assets (including life insurance) exceeding $1 million. When the husband dies, everything goes to his wife tax free. The tax problem arises when the wife dies and can claim only one deduction. If a couple has $2 million in assets when the second spouse dies in 2002 or 2003, the estate

TABLE 11.1 Estate Tax Exemptions

Year of Death	Estate Tax Exemption
2002	$1,000,000.00
2003	$1,000,000.00
2004	$1,500,000.00
2005	$1,500,000.00
2006	$2,000,000.00
2007	$2,000,000.00
2008	$2,000,000.00
2009	$3,500,000.00

would have to pay $435,000 in federal estate taxes—if only sweetheart wills are in place.

If that sounds like a lot, it's because the federal estate tax ranges from 41 to 50 percent. If both spouses had put their assets in trust, they would get two exemptions instead of one and pay no taxes, thereby saving $435,000.

The estate tax picture has become highly confused in recent years. After increasing the estate tax exemption to as much as $3.5 million for deaths occurring in 2009, the Tax Act of 2001 provided that the estate tax be repealed for deaths occurring only in 2010. Perplexingly, the Tax Act of 2001 then provides through a "sunset" provision that the tax changes will expire in 2011 unless reenacted by Congress. If Congress does not amend or reenact the Tax Act of 2001, then the $1 million estate tax exemption is to be reinstated for deaths occurring on or after 2011.

To avoid probate, a couple must transfer their assets into their trusts. The transfers of money or property involve a process called "retitling." The idea is to divide the couple's assets as equally as possible into the two trusts. For instance, a joint brokerage account that reads "John and Mary Jones" would be divided and changed to "John Jones, Revocable Trust" and "Mary Jones, Revocable Trust," thus shifting those assets into two trusts. The deed for a house that is owned jointly also would be revised, Macdonald said. The house could be put into the trust of the spouse with the lesser amount of total assets. But both spouses would retain the same rights to use the house, or even sell it, as before.

When Sara and I did our trusts, we put one-half of our condominium apartment in her trust, one-half in my trust. We retitled our brokerage account, but not our IRA accounts. If I were to die first, Sara would be allowed to roll over my IRAs into her IRAs, so no retitling would be necessary. I could do the same if she were to die first.

While trusts make a lot of sense, they have a few drawbacks. Typically, it costs $2000 to $3000 to have an estate-planning lawyer set up trusts for a married couple and do some of the legal work that goes with it. And the job of retitling assets can be complicated and time consuming. Worse, it may make some people feel that they've lost control of their assets, even though they haven't. In our case, the retitling procedure was a bit tedious, but it was completed in a couple of months.

One of the main arguments for creating a trust is to avoid the time and expense of probate. But many states now have adopted a fast-track system for probate, especially for small estates, and that has made the process easier.

Would it be worthwhile for you to create a bypass trust? That depends on the size of your estate. The magic number is $1 million in 2002 or 2003. If you're close to it or over it, then the trust would be useful. If you have much less, it may not be worth it. Check with an estate planner to make sure.

As I've said, the per-person exemption will be increased gradually to $3.5 million by 2009. Nevertheless, estate taxes still will be due on any assets above that amount.

Getting yourself organized

How do you know what your estate is worth? Here's my two-step plan for measuring the value of your estate and organizing your financial information:

Step One. Take a personal financial inventory by adding up everything you own and everything you owe. If you're married, make three lists. First, list the assets and liabilities that are in your name only; then list those in your spouse's name only; finally, list those assets which you own jointly. When you're done, subtract what is owed from what is owned on all three lists. That will give you a rough idea of the value of your estate, your spouse's estate, and your shared estate.

Typically, a list of assets will include bank accounts, certificates of deposit, stocks, bonds, and mutual funds. The value of your life insurance also should be listed. Include the fair-market value of your home, car, boat, home furnishings, jewelry, real estate, and pension accounts. A list of liabilities would include any money you owe, including your mortgage, bank loans, car loans, and credit card balances.

Step Two. Think for a moment of how hard it would be for your spouse or your children to find all your personal and financial information if you weren't around. You can spare them a lot of grief by doing the job for them. I suggest keeping your information and documents where they are safe and easy to find. A fireproof file cabinet or home safe may be better than a safe-deposit box.

Start by locating your will and trust documents. If you have prearranged your funeral, include the name and phone number of the funeral home, the agreements you signed, and a record of your payments. Among the documents that should be in your file are the deed to your home or other property you own, the title to your car, and your military discharge and veterans' benefit papers, marriage license, divorce papers, birth certificates, citizenship papers, passports, and immigration papers. Also, you should include your bank, brokerage, and mutual fund account numbers and the addresses or phone numbers of those institutions, as well as your credit card numbers, balances, and phone numbers. Finally, include your Social Security number, the amount of your monthly payments, and, if you have direct deposit, the name of the bank to which the check is sent. Do the same for pension payments.

Make sure that a family member knows where you keep the key to your safe-deposit box and the name of the bank where the box is located. Make a list of what's in your box. Also, list the names, numbers, and details of all your insurance policies, especially life, auto, and homeowners policies. And don't forget health insurance and nursing home policies. Make a list of your doctors and their phone numbers, too. And by the way, once you've done all these things, make sure to tell your spouse, children, or other relatives what you've done and where they can find all the information.

As Sara is fond of saying, "Preparedness is next to godliness."

Thinking about the unthinkable

Unfortunately, when it comes to deciding what will happen to your money and your property after you die, you can do everything right and still come out wrong.

Any lawyer who has practiced estate law for any length of time can tell stories of parents who tried to do the right thing by leaving their money and property to their children in equal shares, believing that the show of fairness would help maintain family harmony after they died. But all too often it doesn't work out that way.

"When it comes to money, family loyalty goes out the window," I was told by Jeffrey L. Condon, a Santa Monica, California, estate lawyer, who talked about the conflicts that can arise after parents die. The children are not just the parents' children anymore, Condon said, "They're people dividing money." And that often makes them behave differently from the way they would if their parents were still alive.

Condon told the story of a couple that left everything they owned equally to their three children. However, years earlier, they had spent $250,000 to send one son to medical school. Another son attended a local junior college, while the daughter did not go to college.

After the parents' death, the discrepancy in education spending caused a rift among the siblings. The brother and sister of the doctor felt that he should give them part of his inheritance to equalize what their parents spent on all three. The doctor disagreed; he no longer speaks to his siblings.

What the parents should have done, Condon said, was to equalize their spending on their children during their lifetime. Parents who occasionally help a child financially tend to forget about unequal treatment, Condon said. "But rest assured, your children haven't forgotten. And they're keeping score." Condon and his father, attorney Gerald M. Condon, told the story in their book *Beyond the Grave: The Right Way and the Wrong Way of Leaving Money to Your Children (and Others)* (New York, NY: Harper Business, 1995).

Family strife can arise out of many inheritance scenarios. Second marriages, especially those involving widows and widowers with grown children, can be disasters waiting to happen. All too often, inheritances wind up in the wrong hands because of poor planning, failure to use the right legal tools, or just plain greed. Lawyers who specialize in wills, trusts, and estate planning say there are many ways to create inheritance problems. But there are also ways to prevent them. Here are a few examples:

Unequal shares

Parents often tell Rhonda Macdonald that they want to leave more money to one child than to another. Usually, the reason given is that one child is very successful and "doesn't need the money," while their other child is relatively poor. When Macdonald hears that, she tries to convince the parents that it's a bad idea to give unequal shares to their offspring simply for economic reasons. "By leaving a smaller share to your successful child, you are punishing him or her for success. And by leaving a greater share to your poorer child, you're rewarding his or her lack of success," Macdonald tells her clients. That argument seems to work, Macdonald said, and few of her clients wind up leaving their children unequal shares for economic reasons.

Second marriages

The classic horror story begins when Dad dies and Mom remarries. Mom and her second husband each have three grown children. They really want to leave their individual wealth to their own children, but they already have put all their savings and property in both names and thus own everything jointly. That means that if the second husband dies before Mom does, all their joint assets will automatically become Mom's property. It will then be up to Mom, in her will, to decide what his children and her children will get. And even if Mom leaves most of her second husband's assets to his children, they will have to wait until she dies to get their inheritance. That could take a long time, and his kids are likely to make a considerable fuss over the delay.

The easiest way to avoid these conflicts, Macdonald said, is for couples to keep their assets in their own names. That allows them to leave their individual money and property to their own children through their wills. If they've already put their assets in both names, they can go back and retitle them.

If Mom will need income to live on after her second husband dies, he can set up a trust for her that contains his assets, Macdonald said. Such a trust is called a "qualified terminable interest property," or QTIP trust. It allows Mom to receive income from her second husband's assets after his death. It can also guarantee that the principal of the trust ultimately will be inherited by the second husband's children, although, once again, they may have to wait until Mom dies.

In some cases, this may not be the complete story. For instance, in Virginia, Maryland, and the District of Columbia, Mom can claim one third of her second husband's assets if he omits her from his will or leaves her less than one third, even if the assets are held in his own name. This privilege can be waived with a premarital agreement.

Watch out for those in-laws

A couple in their eighties, Arthur and Mary, plan to leave their estate to their only son, Roger, who is 55. They hope their son, when he dies, will pass along his inheritance to their grandchildren. But they worry about what will happen if their son dies before his wife, Selma, who would then get her husband's inheritance. They are not sure if Selma actually would pass the inheritance along to the grandchildren. In fact, if Selma remarries, the inheritance could be passed along to her second husband and members of his family, and that's not what the grandparents have in mind.

One way for Arthur and Mary to protect their grandchildren's inheritance, according to Macdonald, is to create a generation-skipping trust, which will ensure that the couple's money goes to their grandchildren at a specified age. Here's how that would work: Their son, Roger, would become the trustee of the trust after the deaths of his mother and father. Roger would get the annual income generated by the trust, or a percentage of the value of the trust each year. Roger could use as much of the principal of the trust as necessary to pay expenses for the health, education, and support of himself and his children.

A generation-skipping trust can have tax advantages. For deaths occurring in 2002 (the amounts change after that), up to $1.1 million can be left in trust for grandchildren from each grandparent. This generation-skipping exemption is indexed for inflation each year. The grandchildren will not have to pay taxes on the money when they receive it.

However, the $1.1 million would be counted as part of Arthur or Mary's estate when the second spouse dies. Taxes would be paid on the total value of the estate, less the individual estate tax exemption of $1 million (for deaths occurring in 2002).

When children owe money to their parents

Anger and confusion are almost inevitable when children borrow money from parents and don't pay it back. After the parents die, it is often unclear how much was borrowed, when and how the loans were to be repaid, and whether interest was to be charged. Worse yet, with the passage of time, children often start to think of the money they borrowed not as loans, but gifts. On top of the confusion, Macdonald said, some of the children are likely to demand that their siblings repay their loans, so that the total inheritance is not reduced by the debts.

Macdonald said she tries to head off these problems by asking clients, when they come in to write their wills, to give her the specific details of any loans they made to their children, so she can include the information in the wills. That way, she said, when the parents die, the terms of the loans will be on record.

Naming the executors and trustees

When parents write their wills and create trusts, they often name children as personal representatives, executors, or trustees, making them responsible for placing a value on the assets of the estate, distributing the assets to the heirs, and filing various documents, including the deceased's final income tax. But how many children in a family should be given this task? The answer, says Macdonald, is "All of them." In Macdonald's experience, the offspring will not be happy if they are left out, no matter where in the world they are. They will want to be part of any decision affecting their inheritance, be it by phone, fax, or e-mail.

This is particularly true, Macdonald said, because executors and trustees are allowed to charge a fee for the work involved in settling their parents' estate. When there is more than one executor or trustee, the fee is shared. If only some of the children are named as executors and if they opt to receive executors' fees, Macdonald said, that may skew what otherwise would have been an equal division of assets among the children.

Getting the business

At times, parents flatly refuse to give equal shares of their estate to all their children. Often, that occurs when there is a family business. On those occasions, Macdonald said, parents may insist on leaving the firm to the offspring who have been working with them in the business for years. That may make the other children in a family unhappy, even though they chose to work in other fields. Indeed, those children might even sue on the grounds that they are getting a smaller inheritance than their siblings. If the parents think that such a lawsuit is likely, Macdonald said, they can attempt to head it off by inserting a "no contest" clause in their wills. Under that clause, if the children sue, they lose the inheritance they were slated to get. "If they sue, they get nothing," Macdonald said.

Disinheriting children

There are lots of reasons parents want to omit children from their wills or inheritance plans. The most common one is that a child is estranged and the parents haven't seen him or her for years; in some instances, the child has been involved with alcohol or drugs or has been in trouble with the law.

Jeffrey and Gerald Condon caution parents that if they omit a child from their will, one of two things is likely to happen: The child will either sue or become a burden to his or her siblings. Although such lawsuits generally fail, they can be costly to the other children. In fact, the Condons noted, the other children may find it cheaper to settle than pay the legal costs involved.

Instead of cutting a child out of their will, the Condons advise, parents should put the child's share of the estate in a trust. The parents can then specify when and how their estranged son or daughter will get any money or income from the trust. The Condons also recommend that if parents omit a child from their wills, they should write a letter telling the child what they're doing. The letter may encourage the child to renew his or her ties with the family. At least, they say, it will give the child fair warning of what is going to happen.

Talking it out

Most lawyers agree that whatever inheritance or estate plan you adopt, it is important to explain your actions by discussing them with your children and with other relatives. Children should know exactly what their parents intend to do with their money and other assets. If they have problems with the parents' plans, it's a good idea to find that out before it's too late.

For more information

Here are just a few of the many sources of guidance on wills, trusts, and taxes:

Books

AARP. *Wills & Living Trusts.* Published by AARP. For a free copy, send a postcard to AARP Fulfillment EEO1349, 601 E St. N.W., Washington, DC 20049. Request publication D14535.

American Bar Association. *The American Bar Association Guide to Wills and Estates.* Times Books/Random House, New York, NY, 1995.

Bambord, Jane, et al. *Consumer Reports Money Book.* Consumer Reports Books, Yonkers, NY. The book has a chapter on wills and trusts.

Cane, Michael Allan. *The Five-Minute Lawyer's Guide to Estate Planning."* Dell, New York, NY, 1995.

Maple, Stephen M. *The Complete Idiot's Guide to Wills and Estates.* Alpha Books, New York, NY, 1997.

Rottenberg, Dan. *The Inheritor's Handbook: A Definitive Guide for Beneficiaries.* Bloomberg Press, Pinceton, NJ, 1999

Schumacher, Vickie and Schumacher, Jim. *Understanding Living Trusts: How You Can Avoid Probate, Save Taxes and Enjoy Peace of Mind.* Schumacher Publishing, Los Angeles, CA, 1996.

WEB SITES

National Association of Financial and Estate Planning: www.nafep.com (Click on "Estate Planning.")

Nolo Press: www.nolo.com (Under "Law Centers," click on "Wills and Estate Planning.")

DECISION 12

How can I age successfully?

At some point in our lives, we all have to admit to ourselves that we are growing older. Signs of aging creep up on us in subtle ways. Gray hairs show up in our thirties. We need bifocals in our forties, a hearing aid in our fifties, and a heart bypass operation in our sixties. And then we start to have memory lapses. While they are merely annoying in our younger years, these lapses become scarier as we age.

In a way, even retirement is a sign of aging—not a physical one, perhaps, but an event that is usually related to increasing age. Whether we choose to retire at 62, at 65, or at 70, retirement usually occurs when we have completed about three quarters of our life span. Thus, when we retire, it is clear that we're moving into the final quarter of our lives.

That is not meant to sound grim. In any football game, the last quarter is often the most exciting. So, too, with retirement. It is one more chance to add points on the scoreboard of your life. It is, in fact, a very special time of life, as many retirees have discovered. Indeed, in a recent survey for the National Council on the Aging, 49 percent of Americans age 65 to 69 said, "These are the best years of my life."

I can relate to that sentiment. The opportunity to write the "Retirement Journal" column after I retired—and its popularity— has been the frosting on the cake of my career. Even the chance to put my ideas and experiences together in this book was a long-cherished ambition, realized at age 73. Yes, the clock is ticking. But it can tick for many years. As retirees, our primary challenge is to stay healthy long enough to enjoy the pleasures and opportunities that retirement can bring us.

Thanks to modern medicine and rising living standards, increases in life expectancy have been dramatic. As noted earlier, a 65-year-old woman can expect to live to 84, while a 65-year-old man can look forward to living until 81. Medical advances are steadily extending those frontiers. Living to 100 will soon be commonplace. But what does it take to reach those extended ages? As gerontologists and social scientists learn more about the aging process, they are able to provide us with increasingly better answers to that question.

I found some interesting ideas in a book about growing older, *Successful Aging*, by John W. Rowe and Robert L. Kahn. The book is based on the MacArthur Foundation Study of Aging in America, which took 10 years and cost $15 million. Among other things, the study looked closely at the history and habits of people who were aging well.

The book contains lots of good news for people in their sixties and seventies. The MacArthur study explodes many of the myths about aging and shows that, with proper diet, exercise, and medical care, elderly people can remain physically active and mentally alert for many years. Successful aging, the authors say, is based on three characteristics:

- A low risk of disease and disease-related disability
- High mental and physical abilities
- The desire to remain actively engaged with people

While heredity plays a role in longevity, the authors report that individual lifestyle choices and behavior over many years have the most influence on whether one ages well. Better yet, the authors tell us, it is never too late to change one's lifestyle for the better.

The lesson here is quite clear: The best way to prepare for a healthy old age is to follow a healthy lifestyle while you're young. But even if you didn't do that—I didn't start thinking about my health until I was in my fifties—there's still time.

Confronting illness

While there are many things we can do to preserve our health during retirement, we can't always avoid illness, which often strikes unexpectedly. I know this both from my own experience and from watching the ebb and flow of life in my retirement community, in which the average age is about 70 or 75. Hardly a month goes by that we don't hear about a friend or neighbor who has suffered a heart attack or a stroke or who has developed cancer.

In fact, I had my own medical battle, as I mention briefly in Chapter 8. Shortly after I retired, I decided that it was time to get a long-postponed physical checkup. The checkup led to the discovery of several clogged blood vessels in my heart. Although they had been partially cleared by angioplasty 10 years earlier, the blood vessels were now clogged again. My doctors said a four-way heart bypass operation was necessary.

I agreed to have the surgery. But the whole idea of having to undergo a serious operation so soon after I retired seemed truly unfair. I had worked for almost 45 years, and when I finally felt I was ready to retire, my health and, perhaps, my life seemed to be in jeopardy.

The experience of going through open-heart surgery—and its aftermath—forced me to confront my own mortality in a way I had never done before. I wondered how long my retirement might last. And I asked myself, Even if I survive, what will be the quality of my life?

Fortunately, I recovered from my surgery within a few months, but the experience left me feeling that if there was anything I wanted to do in retirement, I should do it quickly. This sense that my life might be limited was intensified by my wife's medical experience. Three years before my surgery, Sara underwent breast cancer surgery. She recovered after a nine-month ordeal involving chemotherapy. After her recovery, she decided to retire from her job at GE, where she had spent 22 years.

Thus, Sara and I both entered our retirement years after confronting major medical challenges. Sooner than most retirees, we had learned the truth of the old saying, "With good health, everything is possible. Without it, nothing is possible."

Age 74 and pumping iron

After my heart surgery, my doctor sent me to a nearby cardiac rehabilitation center to improve my physical condition. It was there that I learned both aerobics and weight lifting. The first few weeks were rough, because my muscles were weak and my stamina was limited. But I slowly gained back my strength, and my physical condition improved. Five years later, I still invest time and energy in exercise. I tell my friends, especially those who trade stocks, that exercise is one of the few investments I've ever made that seems to have all upside and no downside.

In fact, until I went to the cardiac center, I didn't understand how easy it is to get hooked on regular exercise. My discovery came about this way: The center was open three days a week: Mondays, Wednesdays, and Fridays. So I would go to the center on those days and work out for about two hours a day. But after about four weeks at the center, I noticed something strange. On Tuesdays and Thursdays, I would wake up feeling restless. I wanted to exercise, but the center was closed. So I began making up my own exercises.

I soon figured out what was happening: Exercise had become habit forming. And when I didn't exercise, my body missed it. Later, I read that natural chemicals called endorphins are released in the body during vigorous exercise. Endorphins can make us feel good and can even produce a feeling of euphoria—a feeling sometimes called "runner's high."

I don't know whether other people can get hooked on exercise as easily as I did. But the daily desire to work out made it much easier to get out of bed in the morning and go to the exercise room. I never had to fight the feeling of "Aw, skip it and go back to bed."

After I "graduated" from the cardiac center, I began to work out in the exercise room in our retirement community. The fitness center is located next door to our apartment building. In fact, it is so close that I'd have a hard time thinking of an excuse not to go regularly. Many of my fellow residents also use the exercise room, which was expanded recently because it is so popular. Until I retired, I had no idea that so many retirees devoted part of each day to exercise.

My routine is fairly simple: I walk a mile on the treadmill, in about 20 minutes. Then I spend 10 minutes on the rowing machine, 10 minutes on the stair climber, and about 20 minutes lifting dumbbells and working on the weight machines. As I work out, I see that many of my companions are walking faster, climbing higher, and lifting heavier weights than I do. But I feel no sense of competition. Many of these men and women are in their seventies and eighties, and I can only marvel at their determination to maintain their physical fitness.

Often, people who use the exercise room are recuperating from strokes, heart surgery, knee and hip replacements, and other assorted ailments. Others swim laps in the indoor swimming pool. Some do both.

For many residents, walking is the main form of exercise. On any decent day, the sidewalks and paths of my retirement community are crowded with walkers. A popular pastime is "walking the circle," the circle being a 3.2-mile path that goes around the community.

Some of my retired friends are "mall walkers." Each morning, they drive to a nearby indoor mall, walk rapidly around the shopping area for about an hour, and then gather for coffee and gossip. In inclement weather, I often hear the footsteps of the "hall walkers," residents of our building who get their exercise by walking up and down the corridors and steps of our 10-story building. I've done it; it takes about 45 minutes, and it makes for vigorous exercise.

Having discovered exercise late in life, I have no illusions about how I look when I'm lifting those dumbbells. When I glance in the wall mirror and see this gray-haired, 74-year-old man pumping iron, it's hard to keep from smiling. The sight reminds me of that old magazine ad for bodybuilder Charles Atlas, who boasted that he went from a "97-pound weakling" to "The World's Most Perfectly Developed Man." The ad featured a cartoon of a skinny kid on a beach who loses his girl to a sand-kicking muscleman and resolves to take weight-lifting lessons. As I struggle to lift those weights aloft, I sometimes hear myself saying, as did that kid, "Nobody's going to kick sand in my face!"

Do I wish I had started down the athletic trail 40 years ago? Yes, I do. But it wasn't as though I was a couch potato all my life. As a political reporter and columnist early in my career, I spent years running for campaign planes, trains, and buses. As a homeowner, I spent years mowing lawns, raking leaves, shoveling snow, and painting the house. Sure, it was all work, but it wasn't the kind of regular daily exercise that keeps your muscles toned and your heart healthy. If I had it to do over, I would make more time for exercise, especially because I've learned that exercise not only is good for your muscles but also is good for your brain. And what is good for your brain is good for your memory. And that's worth remembering.

My memory and me

The one thing that frightens me most about growing older is the idea that I might lose my memory. In fact, of all the questions I hear people ask about aging, the most frequent one is, "What's happening to my memory?" If you have ever watched a friend or loved one slip into Alzheimer's or dementia, as I have, you know the horror of watching the erosion of the human mind. I guess if I had a choice, I would prefer almost any other medical problem to losing my mental abilities. I'm sure many people feel the same way.

Memory is such an integral part of our personalities and individuality that it is unsettling to see signs that our memories are failing. In fact, not long ago, I began worrying about my memory after several incidents:

- I was shopping at the local mall when I ran into a man I'd worked with for many years, but I simply couldn't remember his name. It was on the tip of my tongue, but I couldn't dredge it out of my memory. I was embarrassed not to be able to call him by name.

- Another day, I drove to the supermarket, but when I came out, I couldn't remember where I had parked my car. I finally found it after wandering around for several minutes, but I was annoyed with myself.

- While at home, I walked from the kitchen into the bedroom to take care of a small chore. But when I got to the bedroom, I couldn't remember why I had gone in there. So I went back into the kitchen and remembered what I wanted to do in the bedroom.

- I took a phone message for my wife from her sister, but didn't write it down because I was sure I would remember it. When Sara came home and asked if anybody had called, I said no. I had completely forgotten about her sister's call. Hours later, I remembered the call.

- Working at my desk, I found myself trying to recall the name of the capital of California. Once again, it was on the tip of my tongue, but it took a full five minutes before "Sacramento" swam into my consciousness.

After that "memorable" week, I started worrying about my memory. "What's going on here?" I asked myself. "Am I losing my memory? Does this have anything to do with my age?"

I took my questions to Marilyn S. Albert, a professor of psychiatry and neurology at Harvard University. Albert is widely regarded as an expert in the field of aging and memory. She was quite reassuring.

"I wouldn't worry," Albert said after I told her about some of my recent memory lapses. Albert suggested a way to tell whether my occasional episodes of forgetfulness were serious or not. She put it this way:

"When you're reminded of the name you forgot or the location of your car, and you can say, 'Yes, of course. That's it,' then you are probably fine. "The real time to worry," she said, is when you find the name you forgot and you don't get the feeling that you knew it all along." I was happy to hear that, especially because I think I'm still in the "I-knew-it-all-along" camp. That little test also will be good news to my friends and acquaintances. Many people who live in my retirement community, I've noticed, are equally forgetful.

In fact, memory lapses are so common among my peers that they've been given a name. They are called "senior moments." If you listen to the conversations in the lobby, the exercise room, or the local clubhouse, you will hear a resident, in the midst of telling a story, pause and try to remember a name, place, or date. When that name, place, or date can't be recalled, the storyteller is likely to try to cover it up by saying, "Oh, oh, I'm having a senior moment." It's usually said with some embarrassment, but no one is critical. The listeners simply nod sympathetically. It has happened to them, too.

Remembering people's names, Albert told me, represents a common difficulty. "We all forget them," she said. Memory, she noted, is embedded within many connections in the brain. The more such pathways, the easier it is to remember a name; the fewer the pathways, the harder it is to retrieve that name.

Names are often hard to remember because it is difficult to make an association with a "John" or a "Mary" when they are only names by themselves. To improve one's memory of a John or a Mary, an individual needs additional images or associations that will help create more pathways in the brain.

Albert said research has shown that there is a link between aging and memory. "We think [the two are] directly related," she said. Memory loss, she added, can be caused by changes in various areas of the brain that result in the loss of nerve cells and the shrinkage of brain tissue. However, Albert added, "The good news is that we have found that the nerve cells in the cortex are retained." The cortex plays a significant role in memory.

"What seems to be pretty clear is that as people get older, they have more trouble learning new information than younger people," Albert said. In addition, older people may be less inclined to think about cues that might help them remember, say, where they parked their cars—something younger people do spontaneously.

But older people can overcome these difficulties by working at remembering—for example, by deliberately fixing the location of their car in their mind before they leave the parking lot. Working at the business of remembering, Albert says, is a valuable strategy for older people. The evidence, Albert notes, is that once older people learn something—and learn it well—"they won't forget it any more rapidly than someone who is younger."

This ability to concentrate, retain information, and recall it, Albert said, is a key measure of the difference between benign and serious memory lapses. "When people are in the early stages of Alzheimer's," she said, "even if they make an extra effort to learn something, they will forget it." Albert estimates that 10 percent of the people in this country who are over age 65 have Alzheimer's. However, the total number of Alzheimer's cases is rising rapidly because the number of Americans over 65 is climbing steadily. The good news is that the scientific and medical communities are working tirelessly to find ways to alleviate, and eventually find a cure for, Alzheimer's.

How to help your memory

In dealing with my moments of forgetfulness, I've found a number of memory aids and behavioral devices that can reduce the frustration of memory lapses. Here are some of the strategies that I use to get through the day:

- *The calendar.* I use a month-at-a-glance calendar with big boxes, so there is plenty of room to write down doctors' appointments, social engagements, upcoming birthdays, etc. Before you make an appointment, make sure to check your calendar to avoid double booking. Then, develop the habit of checking your calendar each evening, so you will know what you have to do tomorrow, where you are going, and what time you are expected.

- *A place for everything.* If you have trouble finding your car or house keys, your watch or sunglasses, do what Sara does. She has a special place for any item she is likely to need, and she makes sure that the item goes back to that special spot. That way, she knows exactly where to find her things and rarely has to search for anything. I'm less successful with that system than she is, but I'm trying.

- *Parking your car.* Many shopping center parking lots have numbered lanes or rows. When you park, make note of your location, and don't hesitate to jot it down. If there is no numbering system, look around and see where you are in relation to the nearest store, and fix that spot in your mind. That way, you'll be able to find your car easily.

- *Things to do.* The single biggest memory aid for both young and old is a list. To remember the things you want to do, make a list. A word of caution, however: One list is useful, but 10 lists only create confusion. When you develop your list, put the items in order of priority. And confine your list to the things you want to accomplish in the next week or 10 days. Once you've crossed off most of your immediate chores, you can start a new list and repeat the process.

- *Remembering names.* This is a tricky business because we know many people and know them under many different circumstances. For casual first-name greetings with neigh-bors, I repeat their names to myself until I'm sure I have them in mind. For family affairs, at which I will see cousins I haven't seen for a long time—and their children, whom I hardly know—I do some serious homework. That often involves making a small chart of the family, the relatives' names, and who belongs to whom. The system usually works—except for my identical twin nephews. I've spent 40 years trying to tell them apart. For a while, only one wore glasses. That helped. But when they both started wearing glasses, I was sunk.

But what did I do about the former coworker I met in the mall, whose name I could not recall? Well, that won't happen again. His name is a lot like that of a famous general, so when I meet him, I'll just think of that general, and I'll be able to come up with his name. As for trying to remember Sacramento, well, sometimes it's easier to look things up than to wait for your memory to supply the information.

- *Keeping your memory in shape.* The best way to do this, the experts say, is to keep *yourself* in good physical shape. Reg-ular exercise and a proper diet will do as much good for your brain as it will for your muscles. It's also a good idea to keep your mind active, whether you play poker, chess, pool, or the stock market. Reading newspapers, magazines, or novels will help keep those brain cells hum-ming, too.
- *Using the buddy system.* Couples or even friends can help one another remember important things. In fact, the other day, Sara suggested, "We should arrange it so that you remember all the things I forget and I'll remember all of the things you forget."

"Great idea," I said, "I'll try to remember that."

Aging and creativity

I found considerable encouragement about growing older from talking with Dr. Gene D. Cohen, director of the Center on Aging, Health and Humanities, at George Washington University in Washington, D.C. Cohen's view is definitely upbeat. He believes that one's later years can be an extremely creative time of life—intellectually, artistically, and socially. He spells out his ideas in a book, *The Creative Age: Awakening Human Potential in the Second Half of Life.*

Cohen talked of several phases of creativity in later life. Among them are the following:

The "liberation phase"

This is a time, Cohen says, "in which creative expression is shaped by a new degree of personal freedom in retirement or the restructuring of the time commitment to family." When retirees have more free time and comfortable incomes, he relates, they often try new things, especially in the field of art. Indeed, he says, the area of folk art is dominated by older people. "For many people," Cohen says, "retirement is like a patron. A patron gives you time to do something other than having to make ends meet."

In the "liberation phase," which Cohen defines as the late fifties to early seventies, people often get a new sense of freedom to speak their minds and to do things that are courageous. Older people have played major roles in world history, Cohen notes. "The greater freedom and courage that many older adults experience," Cohen says, "help explain why a significant number of older adults about or beyond age 70 have assumed the role of 'shapers' or 'shakers' of society." Among those on Cohen's list are Socrates, Copernicus, Galileo, Mahatma Gandhi, Golda Meir, and Nelson Mandela. These movers and shakers fall into what

Cohen calls social creativity with a "big C," but he talked also of social creativity with a "small c," referring to the opportunities that ordinary people have to do extraordinary things for themselves, their families, or their communities.

Cohen recalls that he once did a study of how widows adapted to living alone after their husbands died. He said he was awed by his findings. The women, he said, showed "remarkable growth and resourcefulness." Indeed, he says, they totally smashed that old stereotype that says, "You can't teach an old dog new tricks."

The summing-up phase

This is a time of life, Cohen says, "in which creative expression is shaped by the desire to find larger meaning in the story of our lives and to give in a larger way of the wisdom we have accrued."

"In the role of 'keepers of the culture,'" Cohen says, "the lessons and fortunes of a lifetime are shared through autobiography and personal storytelling, philanthropy, community activism, and volunteerism." Cohen's views should be quite encouraging to anyone approaching his or her sixties or seventies.

Redefining old age

"The picture of late life itself has changed. It is no longer a portrait of passivity, senility, and sexlessness. Today it has become one of activity, vigor, and intellectual robustness." That quote is from Dr. Robert N. Butler, president of the International Longevity Center—USA, Ltd., which is affiliated with the Mount Sinai School of Medicine in New York. In a recent speech, Butler said he foresees a time when many people will live to 100 or beyond, will work until they are 90, and will routinely have multiple careers.

A leader in the fields of gerontology and geriatrics, Butler was the first director of the National Institute of Aging of the National Institutes of Health from 1975 to 1982. In 1976, he won a Pulitzer prize for his book *Why Survive? Being Old in America.* "This is the first time in human history that the prospect of living a long, healthy, and productive life has become reality for the majority of people in most parts of the world. What was the privilege of the few has become the destiny of many," Butler said.

When I talked with Butler, he told me of his great interest in seeing how many older people are busy working either for pay or as volunteers, caring for grandchildren, taking part in physical-fitness programs, and traveling. This national surge of activity, Butler said, is part of "a redefinition of what later life is all about."

No doubt, this redefinition will continue. There are 35 million Americans who are over 65. And 5000 more turn 65 each day. And the baby boomers are still coming down the road. They, too, will give retirement a new meaning.

In my senior community, for instance, I know many people whose motto is "Eat right, exercise, and stay busy." They do. Although it is hard to see oneself as part of a historic mass movement, it's a good feeling to know that Sara and I are among the millions of people who are helping to change the meaning of old age.

The dos and don'ts of growing older

I have always believed that if something is worth doing, it is worth doing well. Golf, for instance, is much more fun when your drives are straight and your putting is accurate. If it takes a few lessons to help you get there—well, it's worth the cost. You can say the same for almost any other endeavor, including growing older.

The difference, of course, is that it is hard to take "aging lessons" in the way that you might take golfing lessons. Actually, it is not hard to foresee the day when "retirement schools" may become as popular as golfing schools. Until then, learning to age gracefully will remain a do-it-yourself business.

As I grow older, and as I watch the behavior of friends and acquaintances of my age, I find myself making lists of the dos and don'ts of growing older. Together, I believe, they form a strategy that can help you age successfully and gracefully. They work for me. Hopefully, they will work for you, too.

The don'ts

- Don't bore your friends and relatives by talking on and on about your health problems. In fact, when somebody asks, "How are you?"—don't tell them.
- Don't tell the same story to the same person more than once. When you repeat your stories over and over, people think you're getting fuzzy.
- Don't neglect old friends, especially the ones who were an important part of your life. Time goes by quickly, and you don't know how many more chances you'll get to visit with those friends.
- Don't let anger rule your life. Avoid confrontation. It's an imperfect world, and people make mistakes, even when they're trying to do their best.
- Don't assume that age makes you wise and that the world is waiting for your advice. If your friends or relatives want advice, they'll ask for it.
- Don't live in the past. The past may be where you are most comfortable, but it's the present that most people—especially your children and grandchildren—really care about.
- Don't miss your opportunities. You wanted to see a baseball game last year, but you never called for tickets. You wanted to see the new art museum in town, but you never

got there. Ask yourself, if you don't do those things now, when will you?

- Don't become a grumpy old man or woman. Cheerful is better. Laugh, and the world will laugh with you. Grump, and you'll grump alone.
- Don't annoy your friends and relatives with your problems. If you need a hearing aid, get a hearing aid, so that you're not always saying, "What?"
- Don't gripe about your birthdays. Enjoy them. Each year is a gift. Growing old is not a right; it's a privilege. Take a lesson from composer and pianist Eubie Blake, who lived to be 100 years old. "If I'd known I was gonna live this long," Blake said, "I'd have taken better care of myself."

The dos

- Do choose a retirement activity you really enjoy. It can be a part-time job, working as a volunteer, a hobby, or even a sport. Make that activity the focus of your life. It's wonderful to be able to spend time doing something you really like.
- Do exercise regularly. It's good for the body, but it's also good for the mind. Exercise helps reduce tension and anxiety and provides a sense of physical well-being.
- Do eat healthfully. Information on good nutrition is all around us. Figure out what foods are best for you, and include them in your daily diet. If you're confused, ask your doctor for advice.
- Do stay tuned into the world around you. It's important to stay mentally alert. Newspapers, books, magazines, and TV shows can keep you up to date on the issues of the day. Think about joining a book club. Buy a computer and get on the Internet.

- Do try to meet new people and develop new friendships. A good way to do that is join a charitable, religious, or civic group. Volunteers are always welcome.

- Do maintain your physical and mental independence. For as long as your health and finances allow, try to handle your own affairs, do things for yourself, and live by your own schedule.

- Do take advantage of your experience and inner strength when personal or family troubles arise. Remember that you've spent a lifetime learning the strategies of survival. Use your knowledge to help yourself and others.

- Do pace yourself as you age. It's okay to walk a bit slower, take more time to go through the supermarket checkout line, and even drive in the slow lane. If other drivers honk at you, let them rush on by.

- Do keep your sense of humor. Make a small mental list of jokes you can tell to friends. As the *Reader's Digest* says, "Laughter is the best medicine."

- Do find a way to be friends with your children and grand-children, even though they are very busy. You need them, and whether they realize it or not, they need you.

A final word

At this point, you might say, "Now that you've told us about all those retirement decisions and dilemmas, tell us, What has retirement been like for you and Sara?" My answer may surprise you, but I am being truthful when I say, "our retirement has been great."

Yes, it did take a lot of effort to get through the retirement process. And yes, I do wish I had planned my retirement with more foresight. But having said that, I can equally well say that the precious thing about retirement is that it has given me time: time to be creative, time to pursue personal goals, and time to see and do some of the things I didn't have time for during my 45 years of working.

In addition to time, retirement has given me some important second chances: the chance to be of service to my community, the chance to explore the neglected frontiers of family and friendships, and, yes, the chance to slow down. Its amazing how good it feels not to be in a hurry all the time, especially when you want to simply pass the time of day with a relative or friend.

Finally, for Sara and me, retirement has been a special time of closeness and joy. We have led productive and exciting lives, and while we cannot predict the future, we look forward to a long and healthy retirement and wish only for the courage to make the most of whatever life brings us in the years ahead. Sara and I hope that our experiences will help you find your way to a happy retirement.

For more information

BOOKS

Cohen, Gene. *The Creative Age: Awakening Human Potential in the Second Half of Life.* Avon Books, New York, NY, 2000.

Hayflick, Leonard. *How and Why We Age.* Ballantine Books, New York, NY, 1994.

Powell, Douglas H. *Nine Myths of Aging: Maximizing the Quality of Later Life.* Thorndike Press, Thorndike, ME, 1998.

Rowe, John W. and Kahn, Robert L. *Successful Aging.* Pantheon Books, New York, NY, 1998.

WEB SITES

AARP: www.aarp.org. AARP's Guide to Internet Resources Related to Aging contains links to many other Web sites, including those related to specific diseases.

Access America for Seniors: www.seniors.gov. This is a federal interagency Web site that offers consumer information from 19 government agencies.

Administration on Aging: www.aoa.dhhs.gov. Information from the federal agency that deals with issues affecting older Americans.

Elder Web: www.elderweb.com. Sources of information for professionals and family caregivers.

Elderhostel www.elderhostel.org. Describes educational and travel programs for seniors at home and abroad.

National Institute on Aging: www.nih.gov/nia/. The latest news on federal research into aging and other age-related activities.

SeniorCom www.senior.com. This site provides a variety of health-related, legal, financial, and other information.

SeniorNet: www.seniornet.org. Founded in 1986, this organization provides computer training for older Americans at 175 centers around the country.

Senior Sites: www.seniorsites.com. Contains a listing of nonprofit providers of senior housing, health care, and services.

Index

About the Author

Stan Hinden writes a syndicated column, "Retirement Journal," in which he discusses the decisions, dilemmas, and challenges of retirement. The column has won honors from the American University School of Communications and the Investment Company Institute for "excellence in personal finance reporting." Before retiring, Stan spent 23 years at the *Washington Post* including a dozen years as a financial reporter and columnist.